StayWell

TABLE OF CONTENTS

AMERICAN RED CROSS FIRST AID/CPR/AED PROGRAM PURPOSE:

Give individuals in the workplace the knowledge and skills necessary to prevent, recognize, and provide basic care for injuries and sudden illnesses until advanced medical personnel arrive and take over.

Section 1: Standard First Aid

Standard First Aid Course and Standard First Aid with AED Training Outline

Topic	Lecture	Video	Adult CPR/AED Skills Card	First Aid Skills Card	Participant's Booklet
Introduction	x	x			page 2
Recognizing Emergencies	x				page 3
Protecting Yourself	x				pages 4-5, 22
Before Providing Care	x				pages 6-8
Prioritizing Care	x	x	x		pages 9-12
Rescue Breathing	x	x	x		page 13
Cardiac Emergencies	x	x	x		
Sudden Illness	x	x			pages 14-15
Wounds	x	x		x	pages 16-19
Injuries to Muscles, Bones, and Joints	x	x		x	page 20
Heat- and Cold-related Emergencies	x	x			page 21
Written Examination	x				pages 23-34

First Aid Course Outline

Topic	Lecture	Video	Adult CPR/AED Skills Card	First Aid Skills Card	Participant's Booklet
Introduction	x	x			page 2
Recognizing Emergencies	x				page 3
Protecting Yourself	x				pages 4-5, 22
Before Providing Care	x				pages 6-8
Prioritizing Care	x	x			pages 9-12
Sudden Illness	x	x			pages 14-15
Wounds	x	x		x	pages 16-19
Injuries to Muscles, Bones, and Joints	x	x		x	page 20
Heat- and Cold-related Emergencies	x	x			page 21
Written Examination	x				pages 23-34

Adult CPR Course Outline

Topic	Lecture	SFA Video	Adult CPR/AED Skills Card	First Aid Skills Card	Participant's Booklet
Introduction	x	x			page 2
Recognizing Emergencies	x				page 3
Protecting Yourself	x				pages 4-5, 22
Before Providing Care	x				pages 6-8
Prioritizing Care	x	x	x		pages 9-12
Rescue Breathing	x	x	x		page 13
Cardiac Emergencies	x	x	x		
Written Examination	x				pages 23-34

RECOGNIZING EMERGENCIES

Recognizing an Emergency

- Emergencies can often be recognized because of unusual sights, appearances or behaviors, odors, and noises.
- It may be challenging to recognize an emergency or sudden illness in some situations. The signals are not always obvious or easy to identify.
  - A victim may deny anything is seriously wrong.
  - If you think something is wrong, check the victim. Ask questions. Questions may help you determine what is wrong.
- Once an emergency has been recognized, be calm and follow the emergency action steps: **CHECK-CALL-CARE.**

CHECK

The scene–for safety, to find out what happened, to determine how many victims there are, and for bystanders who can assist.

The victim–for consciousness.

CALL

9-1-1 or the workplace emergency number.

CARE

For life-threatening conditions.

Check
Call
Care

3

PROTECTING YOURSELF

Good Samaritan Laws

- Good Samaritan laws were enacted in the United States to give legal protection to people who willingly provide emergency care to ill or injured persons without accepting anything in return.

- Good Samaritan laws were enacted to encourage people to help others in emergency situations. They require that the "Good Samaritan" use common sense and a reasonable level of skill, not to exceed the scope of the individual's training in emergency situations. They assume each person would do his or her best to save a life or prevent further injury.

- Good Samaritan laws vary from state to state. If you are interested in finding out about your state's Good Samaritan laws, contact a legal professional or your state Attorney General's office, or check your local library.

Obtaining Consent

Before giving care to a conscious victim you must first get consent. To get consent—

- State your name.
- Tell the victim you are trained in first aid.
- Ask the victim if you can help.
- Explain what you think may be wrong.
- Explain what you plan to do.

Once the victim gives consent, provide the appropriate care.

If the victim does not give consent, do not give care, but still call 9-1-1 or the workplace emergency number.

A victim who is unconscious, confused, or seriously ill may not be able to grant consent. In such cases, consent is implied. Implied consent means that the victim would agree to the care if he or she could.

Preventing Disease Transmission

The risk of getting a disease while giving first aid is extremely rare. The following precautions can reduce the risk even further:

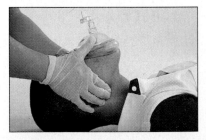

- Avoid contact with blood and other body fluids.
- Use protective equipment, such as disposable gloves and breathing barriers.
- Thoroughly wash your hands with soap and water immediately after giving care.

PROTECTING YOURSELF

Cleaning Up a Blood Spill

If a blood spill occurs—

- Clean up the spill immediately or as soon as possible after the spill occurs.
- Use disposable gloves and other personal protective equipment when cleaning spills.
- Wipe up the spill with paper towels or other absorbent material.
- After the area has been wiped up, flood the area with a solution of 1/4 cup of liquid chlorine bleach to 1 gallon of fresh water, and allow it to stand for at least 20 minutes.
- Dispose of the contaminated material used to clean up the spill in a labeled biohazard container.

Preventing Disease Transmission Quiz

Directions: Read each question and circle whether it is **True** or **False**.

1. **True False** Do not touch your mouth, nose, or eyes when giving first aid.
2. **True False** Avoid touching objects with your skin that may have been in contact with blood or other body fluids.
3. **True False** Cover any cuts, scrapes, or skin irritations prior to using protective equipment.
4. **True False** Only use disposable gloves if you suspect the victim has a disease.
5. **True False** Avoid contact with broken glass, needles, or other sharp objects.
6. **True False** If you come in direct contact with a victim's body fluids while giving first aid, do not tell anybody, especially your supervisor or doctor.
7. **True False** Remove jewelry from your hands before putting on disposable gloves.

OSHA Home Page Address

To get a copy of the OSHA Bloodborne Pathogens Standard (CFR 1910.1030), or if you have further questions regarding the bloodborne pathogens standard, refer to OSHA's web site http://www.osha.gov

BEFORE PROVIDING CARE

Move an Injured Victim Only If—

- The scene is becoming unsafe.
- You have to reach another victim who may have a more serious injury or illness.
- You need to provide proper care (for example, someone has collapsed on a stairway, does not have signs of circulation, and needs CPR. CPR needs to be performed on a firm, flat surface).

Clothes Drag

To move a victim that may have a head, neck, or back injury—
1. Gather the victim's clothing behind the victim's neck.
2. Pull the victim to safety.
3. While moving the victim, cradle the head with the victim's clothes and your hands.

Two-Person Seat Carry

To carry a victim who cannot walk and has no suspected head, neck, or back injury—
1. Put one arm under the victim's thighs and the other across the victim's back.
2. Interlock your arms with those of a second rescuer under the victim's legs and across the victim's back.
3. Move the victim to safety.

Walking Assist

To help a victim who needs assistance walking to safety—
1. Place the victim's arm across your shoulders, and hold it in place with one hand.
2. Support the victim with your other hand around the victim's waist.
3. Move the victim to safety.

Blanket Drag

To move a victim in an emergency situation when equipment is limited—
1. Keep the victim between you and the blanket.
2. Gather half the blanket and place it against the victim's side.
3. Roll the victim as a unit toward you.
4. Reach over and place the blanket so that it will be positioned under the victim.
5. Roll the victim onto the blanket.
6. Gather the blanket at the head and move the victim.

Foot Drag

To move a victim too large to carry or move otherwise—
1. Firmly grasp the victim's ankles and move backwards.
2. Pull the victim in a straight line, and be careful not to bump the victim's head.

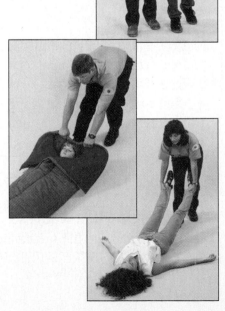

BEFORE PROVIDING CARE

When to Call 9-1-1 Quiz

Directions:

Place a checkmark in the box next to any life-threatening conditions in which 9-1-1 or the workplace emergency number should be called:

- ❑ **Minor bruise on the arm**
- ❑ **Unconsciousness**
- ❑ **Trouble breathing**
- ❑ **Abrasion on the elbow**
- ❑ **Not breathing**
- ❑ **Cut lip**
- ❑ **No signs of circulation**
- ❑ **Persistent chest pain**
- ❑ **Severe bleeding that does not stop**
- ❑ **Mild sunburn on the shoulders**
- ❑ **Cramp in the thigh**
- ❑ **Deep burn to the face and neck**
- ❑ **Pain in the abdomen that does not go away**
- ❑ **Vomiting blood**
- ❑ **Seizures**
- ❑ **Injury to the head**
- ❑ **Appears to have been poisoned**
- ❑ **Splinter in the finger**
- ❑ **Injured arm with bone showing through the skin**
- ❑ **Bloody nose**

NOTE The conditions listed above are not a complete list of life-threatening conditions, and there are always exceptions. If you are confused or unsure about what to do, call 9-1-1 or the workplace emergency number.

7

BEFORE PROVIDING CARE

Emergency Information

Emergency Telephone Numbers

(Dial _____ for outside line)

9-1-1 (or workplace emergency number):_____

Fire: _____

Police: _____

Poison Control Center:_____

Number of this telephone: _____

Other Important Telephone Numbers

Safety Officer: _____

Facility maintenance: _____

Power company:_____

Gas company:_____

Weather bureau:_____

Name and address of medical facility with 24-hour emergency care: _____

Information for Emergency Call

(Be prepared to give this information to the EMS dispatcher.)

- Location
- Street address
- Cross streets
- City or town
- Directions
- Telephone number from which the call is being made
- Caller's name
- What happened
- How many people are injured
- Condition of injured person(s)
- Help (care) being provided

Note: Do not hang up first. Let the EMS dispatcher hang up first.

9-1-1E

In cities with Enhanced (9-1-1E) systems, it is still important to know the information listed above for communication to the dispatcher. In many buildings, the telephone systems may connect through a switchboard that will show only the corporate address rather than the specific facility from which you are calling. With mobile telephones, 9-1-1E is not functional in identifying a fixed location on the dispatcher's screen. Sharing this information is the only way to provide it.

3-1-1

Many 9-1-1 calls in the U.S. are not emergencies. For this reason, some cities have begun to use 3-1-1 as the number for people to call for nonemergency situations. Find out if your area uses this number. Remember, your local emergency number is for just that—emergencies! So please, use good judgment.

PRIORITIZING CARE—ADULT

Prioritizing Care Activity

In an emergency with more than one victim, you may need to prioritize care
(determine who needs help first).

Directions:

Read the following emergency situations. Circle the victim in each emergency situation who
has a life-threatening condition and needs help first.

Emergency Situation—1

You are returning to work from a lunch break when you hear the sound of screeching wheels and then a
crash. There has been a vehicle accident between a car that was leaving the parking lot and a truck.
After checking the scene, you approach to check the victims. Which victim needs help first?

Victim 1 The driver of the truck who gets out to examine the driver and passenger of the car.

Victim 2 The driver of the car who is moaning in pain and appears to have a cut on his face.

Victim 3 The passenger of the car who is not moving at all and appears to be unconscious.

Emergency Situation—2

You are at a construction site when you hear a loud, crashing noise and then some screaming. Part of a
structure and some scaffolding have collapsed, injuring several people. Which victim needs help first?

Victim 1 Who gets up slowly and stumbles away from the debris.

Victim 2 Who is bleeding severely and appears to have a broken arm.

Victim 3 Who is lying on the ground and tells you that her ankle hurts and she may have twisted it.

Emergency Situation—3

You and some co-workers have been working hard outside. It is a hot, humid day and all of you are
exhausted. You take a short break and go to the cooler for some water. When you return, three of your
co-workers are sitting down; they do not look well. One of them tries to stand up but falls over. Which
victim needs help first?

Victim 1 Who fell over and is now sitting on the ground. His skin appears moist and ashen, and he is
sweating profusely.

Victim 2 Who has hot, red, dry skin. He seems semiconscious and does not respond when you ask how
he is feeling.

Victim 3 Who is sweating profusely and his skin appears pale and moist. He is complaining that he is
tired.

PRIORITIZING CARE

Checking a Conscious Victim

First, check the scene. Then, check the victim for life-threatening conditions. Tell the victim not to move, and get consent to help. If there are any life-threatening conditions, call 9-1-1 or your workplace emergency number. If there are no life-threatening conditions and the victim is conscious—

ASK THE VICTIM—

- What happened?
- Do you feel pain anywhere?
- Do you feel numbness or loss of sensation?
- Do you have any allergies?
- Do you have any medical conditions or are you taking any medications?
- When did you last eat or drink anything?

Give this information to EMS personnel when they arrive.

CHECK THE VICTIM FROM HEAD TO TOE:

- Begin the check at the top of the head, face, ears, nose, and mouth. Look for cuts, bruises, bumps, depressions, bleeding, or fluid.
- Feel the victim's forehead with the back of your hand.
- Look at the coloring of the victim's face and lips.
- Notice how the skin looks and feels.
- Look over the body.
- Watch the victim for signals of pain and listen for sounds of pain.
- Watch for changes in consciousness and breathing.
- When the check is complete, if the victim can move without any pain and there are no other signs of injury, have the victim rest comfortably.

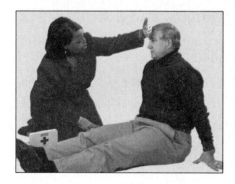

CARING FOR SHOCK

- The signals of shock are—
  - Restlessness or irritability.
  - Nausea and vomiting.
  - An altered level of consciousness.
  - Pale or ashen, cool, moist skin.
  - A blue tinge to lips and nailbeds.
  - Rapid breathing and rapid pulse.
- After caring for the life-threatening emergency, provide care for shock to help minimize its effects.

10

PRIORITIZING CARE

Checking a Conscious Victim

TAKE STEPS TO MINIMIZE THE EFFECTS OF SHOCK:

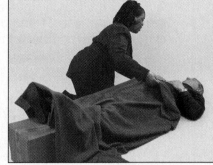

- Make sure 9-1-1 or the workplace emergency number has been called.
- Continue to monitor the victim's airway, breathing, and circulation (ABCs).
- Control any external bleeding.
- Keep the victim from getting chilled or overheated.
- Elevate the legs about 12 inches if a head, neck, or back injury or broken bones in the hips or legs are not suspected.
- Comfort and reassure the victim until advanced medical personnel arrive and take over.

Do not give food or drink to the victim.

Checking an Unconscious Victim

1. Check the scene for safety, then check the victim.

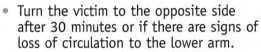

- Turn the victim to the opposite side after 30 minutes or if there are signs of loss of circulation to the lower arm.

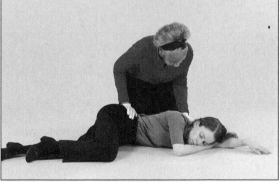

2. Tap the victim's shoulder and shout to see if the victim responds.

3. If the victim does not respond...Call, or have someone else call, 9-1-1 or the workplace emergency number.

4. Without moving the victim, look, listen, and feel for breathing for about 5 seconds.

5. If the victim is unconscious, but is breathing and has signs of circulation (normal breathing, coughing or movement in response to rescue breaths, a pulse)... Place him or her in the recovery position.

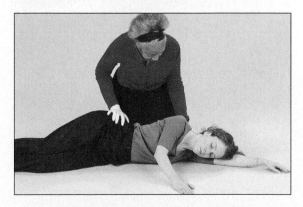

6. Or, if the victim is not breathing or you cannot tell...Roll the victim onto the back, while supporting the head and neck.

11

Tip: Apply basic precautions to prevent disease transmission. Use protective equipment (disposable gloves/breathing barriers). Wash your hands immediately after giving care.

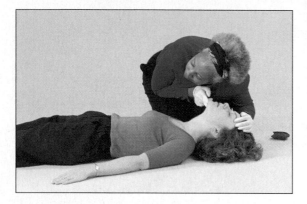

7. Tilt the head back and lift the chin to open the airway.
   • Look, listen, and feel for breathing for about 5 seconds.

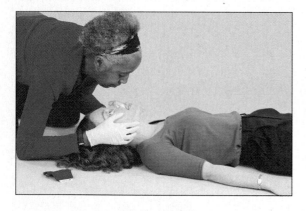

Tip: If you suspect a head, neck, or back injury, you can use the jaw thrust maneuver. Minimize movement of the head and neck when opening the airway.

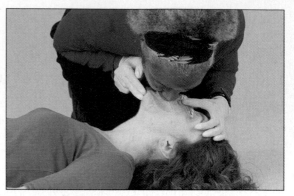

8. If the victim is not breathing...Give 2 rescue breaths.
   • Tilt the head back and lift the chin to open the airway.
   • Pinch the nose shut.
   • Breathe slowly into the victim.

If breaths do not go in, the victim may have an airway obstruction. You can learn how to remove an airway obstruction in any American Red Cross CPR class; ask your instructor for details on how to sign up for these classes after your class.

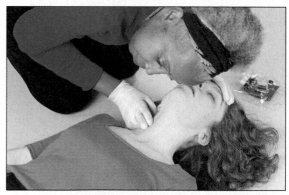

9. If breaths go in...Check for signs of circulation.
   • Find the Adam's apple and slide your fingers toward you and down into the groove at the side of the neck.
   • Check for signs of circulation for no more than 10 seconds.

RESCUE BREATHING

Special Situations

Vomiting

Care

If the victim begins to vomit, remove the breathing barrier, then...

1. Turn the victim's head and body together as a unit to the side.
2. Wipe out the victim's mouth with your finger.
3. Carefully reposition the victim on his or her back.
4. Replace the breathing barrier.
5. Open the airway.
6. Continue with rescue breathing as needed.

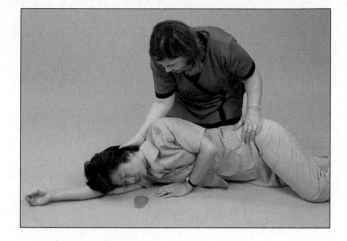

Drowning

Care

If the victim is unconscious and not breathing...

1. Attempt rescue breathing.
2. If air does not go in, reposition the airway and give breaths again.
3. If breaths do not go in, give care for unconscious choking.
4. Once the airway is clear, provide rescue breathing or CPR as needed.

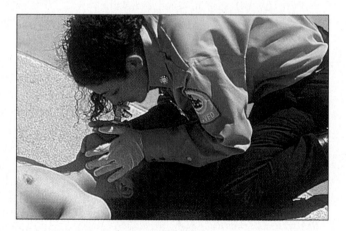

SUDDEN ILLNESS

Signals of Sudden Illness

You may not know the exact cause of a sudden illness, but this should not keep you from providing care. Generally, victims of sudden illness look and feel ill. If you think something is wrong, check the victim. A victim may deny anything is seriously wrong. Do not be afraid to ask the victim questions. The victim's condition can worsen rapidly if not cared for.

Caring for Sudden Illness Activity
Directions:

Match each sudden illness in the first column with the appropriate care steps in the second column. Write the letter of the correct care steps on the line next to the sudden illness.

<table>
<tr><th>Sudden Illness</th><th>Care Steps</th></tr>
<tr><td>

STROKE _D_

- Confusion, dizziness, or disorientation
- Trouble breathing
- Paralysis to the face, arm, or leg; usually on one side
- Difficulty with speech, vision, or walking
- Severe headache

</td><td>

A
- Call 9-1-1 or the workplace emergency number.
- Follow basic precautions for preventing disease transmission.
- Care for life-threatening conditions.
- Continue to monitor the airway, breathing, and circulation.
- Keep the victim comfortable.
- Do not induce vomiting unless directed to.

</td></tr>
<tr><td>

SEIZURE _C_

- Confusion, dizziness, or disorientation
- Trouble breathing
- Body may stiffen
- Convulsions
- After convulsions—
  - Relaxed state
  - Tired and confused
  - Headache

</td><td>

B
- Call 9-1-1 or the workplace emergency number.
- Follow basic precautions for preventing disease transmission.
- Care for life-threatening conditions.
- Continue to monitor the airway, breathing, and circulation.
- Keep the victim comfortable.
- If conscious, give the victim some form of sugar.

</td></tr>
<tr><td>

DIABETIC EMERGENCY _B_

- Confusion, dizziness, or disorientation
- Trouble breathing
- Deep, rapid breaths
- Convulsions

</td><td>

C
- Call 9-1-1 or the workplace emergency number.
- Follow basic precautions for preventing disease transmission.
- Care for life-threatening conditions.
- Continue to monitor the airway, breathing, and circulation.
- Keep the victim comfortable.
- Do not give the victim anything to eat or drink.
- Cushion the victim's head.
- Remove any nearby objects that may cause injury.

</td></tr>
<tr><td>

POISONING/ALLERGIC REACTION _A_

- Confusion, dizziness, or disorientation
- Trouble breathing
- Coughing
- Back pain
- Abnormal pulse rate
- Sweating

</td><td>

D
- Call 9-1-1 or the workplace emergency number.
- Follow basic precautions for preventing disease transmission.
- Care for life-threatening conditions.
- Continue to monitor the airway, breathing, and circulation.
- Keep the victim comfortable.
- Do not give the victim anything to eat or drink.

</td></tr>
</table>

14

SUDDEN ILLNESS

Bites and Stings

Spiderbites/Scorpion Stings

There are only two spiders in the United States whose bite can make you seriously sick or can be fatal—the black widow and the brown recluse. Spiderbites usually occur on the hands and arms of people reaching into places such as wood, rock, and brush piles or rummaging in dark areas.

Only a few species of scorpions have a sting that can cause death. If you think someone has been bitten by a black widow or brown recluse or stung by a scorpion, wash the wound, apply a cold pack to the site, and get medical help immediately.

Snakebites

Snakebites kill very few people in the United States. Of the 8,000 people bitten annually in the United States, less than 12 die. Rattlesnakes account for most of the snakebites and snakebite deaths. To care for someone bitten by a snake, wash the wound, immobilize the injured area, keeping it lower than the heart, if possible, and call 9-1-1 or your workplace emergency number.

Stings

Insect stings are painful and can be fatal. Some people have severe allergic reactions to insect stings. This allergic reaction may result in a breathing emergency. If someone is having a breathing emergency, call 9-1-1 or your workplace emergency number.

15

WOUNDS

First Aid Kit

- Store your first aid kit in a convenient area so that it is readily available for use.
- First aid supplies should be checked and restocked regularly.
- Consider some of the pictured items for your first aid kit, as well as other supplies that may be appropriate for your workplace.

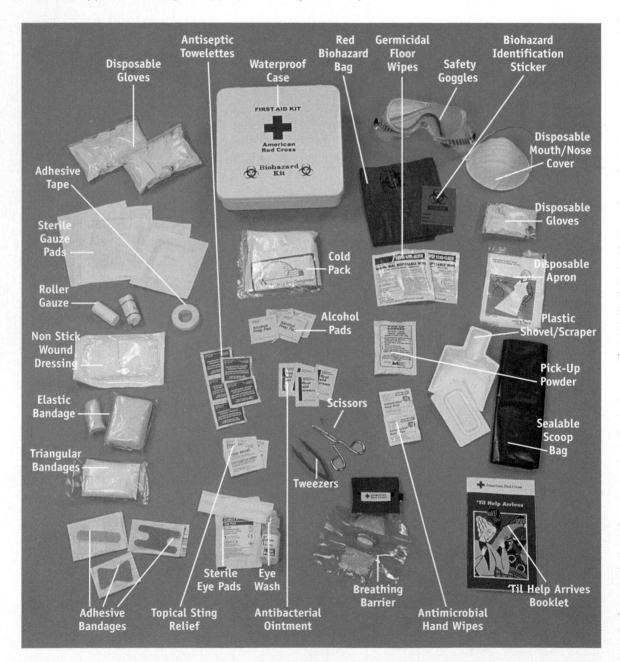

WOUNDS

Care for Special Situations—Bleeding

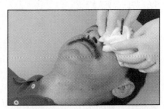

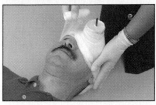

Eye Injury
- Place the victim in a comfortable position.
- Do not attempt to remove any object embedded in the eye.
- Place a sterile dressing around the object.
- Stabilize the object as best you can.
- Apply a bandage.
- ***Never put direct pressure on the eyeball.***

Injuries to the Mouth and Teeth

- To control bleeding inside the cheek, place folded dressings inside the mouth against the wound.
- To control bleeding on the outside of the cheek, use dressings to apply pressure directly to the wound and bandage it so as not to restrict breathing.

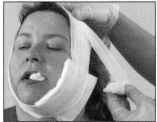

- If a tooth is knocked out, place a sterile dressing directly in the space left by the tooth. Have the victim bite down gently to apply direct pressure.
- Preserve the tooth by placing it in a closed container of cool, fresh milk. If milk is not available, use water. Always try to handle the tooth by the crown (chewing edge) and not the root. Get the victim and the tooth to a dentist as soon as possible.

Abdomen

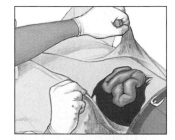

- Wounds that break through the abdominal wall can cause organs to push out.
- Carefully remove clothing from around the wound.
- Do not attempt to put the organs back into the abdomen.
- Cover the organs with a moist, sterile dressing and cover the dressing with plastic wrap.
- Place a folded towel or cloth over the dressing to keep the organs warm.
- Care for shock.

Nosebleed

- Lean forward.
- Pinch the nostrils together until bleeding stops.

WOUNDS

Care for Special Situations—Bleeding

Severed Body Parts
- Control bleeding.
- Wrap a severed body part(s) in gauze (or clean material), put in a plastic bag, and put the bag on ice.
- Care for shock.
- Be sure the part is taken to the hospital with the victim immediately.

Animal Bites

If the bleeding is minor—
- Wash the wound with soap and water.
- Control bleeding.
- Cover with a sterile bandage.
- Call 9-1-1 or the workplace emergency number if the wound bleeds severely or if you suspect the animal has rabies.

Pregnancy

If a woman is giving birth—
- Call 9-1-1 or the workplace emergency number.
- Important information to give the dispatcher:
  - Her name, age, and expected due date
  - How long she has been having labor pains
  - If this is her first child
- Talk with the woman to help her remain calm.
- Place layers of newspaper covered with layers of linens, towels, or blankets under her.
- Control the scene so that the woman will have privacy.
- Position the woman on her back with her knees bent, feet flat, and legs spread wide apart.
- Remember, the woman delivers the baby, so be patient and let it happen naturally.
- The baby will be slippery; avoid dropping the baby.
- Keep the baby warm.

NOTE—
- *Do not let the woman get up or leave to find a bathroom (most women have a desire to use the restroom).*
- *Do not hold her knees together; this will not slow the birth process and may complicate the birth or harm the fetus.*
- *Do not place your fingers in the vagina for any reason.*
- *Do not pull on the baby.*

Embedded Objects
- Place several dressings around the object to keep it from moving.
- Bandage the dressings in place around the object.
- *Do not remove the object.*

18

WOUNDS

Burn Activity

Directions:

Write down how you would respond to the following situations in the space provided.

- ### Scenario 1

  A co-worker drops a bottle that contains a chemical agent. The bottle hits the edge of the counter and breaks. The chemical agent splashes on your co-worker's exposed skin on her arm. The chemical agent is burning her skin. What care would you give?

  _____

  _____

  _____

  _____

- ### Scenario 2

  Today your office is having a going away party and barbecue for one of your co-workers. While a co-worker is putting the lighter fluid on the charcoal, someone throws a match into the barbecue pit. The person with the lighter fluid screams as his hand and arm catch fire. You put the fire out by using your jacket. When you remove the jacket, you notice that his arm has deep burns with blisters. What care would you give?

  _____

  _____

  _____

  _____

- ### Scenario 3

  At your worksite, an electrician puts his hand on a live fuse box and gets electrocuted. He is thrown back several feet and has a severe charred burn on his hand. He is lying on the ground and is unconscious. What care would you give?

  _____

  _____

  _____

  _____

19

INJURIES TO MUSCLES, BONES, AND JOINTS

Caring for Muscle, Bone, and Joint Injuries

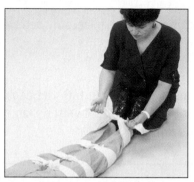

Leg Injury
Immobilize an injured leg by binding it to the uninjured leg.

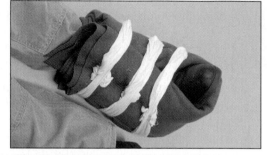

Foot Injuries
Immobilize the ankle and foot by using a soft splint, such as a pillow or rolled blanket. Do not remove the shoes.

Rib/Breastbone Fracture
Place a pillow or folded blanket between the injured ribs and the arm. Bind the arm to the body to help support the injured area.

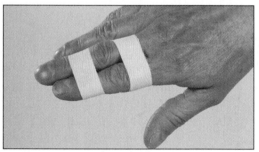

Hand and Finger Injuries
Apply a bulky dressing to the injured area. For a possible fractured or dislocated finger, tape the injured finger to a finger next to it.

Check
Call
Care

Open Fracture

An open fracture occurs when a bone is severely injured, causing the bone ends to tear through the skin and surrounding tissue. To care for a victim with an open fracture—

- Place sterile dressings around the open fracture as you would for an embedded object.
- Bandage the dressings in place around the fracture.
- Avoid moving the exposed bone and limb; this may cause the victim a great deal of pain and may complicate recovery.

HEAT- AND COLD-RELATED EMERGENCIES

HEAT-RELATED EMERGENCIES

Signals	Care
Heat Cramps • Painful muscle spasms, usually in the legs and abdomen	• Have the victim move to a cool place. • Give cool water to drink. • Have the victim lightly stretch the muscle and gently massage the area.
Heat Exhaustion • Cool, moist, pale, flushed, or ashen skin • Headache, nausea, dizziness • Weakness, exhaustion	• Move the victim to a cooler environment. • Loosen or remove clothing. • Fan the victim. • Get the victim into circulating air while applying water with a cloth or sponge. • If the victim is conscious, give small amounts of cool water to drink. • If the victim's condition does not improve or if you suspect heat stroke, call 9-1-1 or the workplace emergency number.
Heat Stroke • A change in the level of consciousness • High body temperature • Red, hot skin that can be either dry or moist • Rapid or weak pulse • Rapid or shallow breathing	• Call 9-1-1 or the workplace emergency number. • Give care until help arrives by following the care steps above for heat exhaustion.

COLD-RELATED EMERGENCIES

Signals	Care
Hypothermia • Shivering • Slow, irregular pulse • Numbness • Glassy stare • Apathy or impaired judgement • Loss of muscle control, no shivering, or loss of consciousness (late stages of hypothermia)	• Gently move the victim to a warm place. • Check ABCs and care for shock. • Remove wet clothing and cover the victim with blankets and plastic sheeting to hold in body heat from shivering. • Warm the victim slowly and handle the victim carefully.
Frostbite • Loss of feeling and sensation in the extremity • Discolored, waxy skin appearance • Severe frostbite may include blisters and blue skin	• Remove wet clothing and jewelry from the affected area. • Soak the frostbitten area in warm water. • Cover with dry, sterile dressings—do not rub anything on the area. • Check ABCs and care for shock. • Do not rewarm a frostbitten part if there is a danger of it refreezing.

21

Removing Disposable Gloves

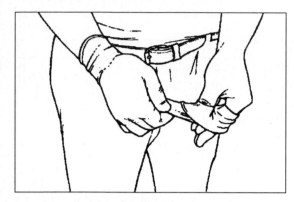

Partially remove first glove

- Pinch glove at the wrist, being careful to touch only the glove's outside surface.
- Pull glove toward the fingertips without completely removing it.
- The glove is now inside out.

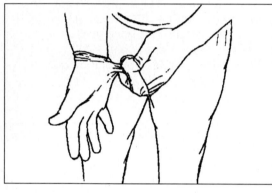

Remove second glove

- With partially gloved hand, pinch the exterior of second glove.

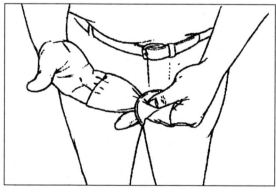

- Pull the second glove toward the fingertips until it is inside out, then remove it completely.

Finish removing both gloves

- Grasp both gloves with your free hand.
- Touch only the clean interior surface of the glove.

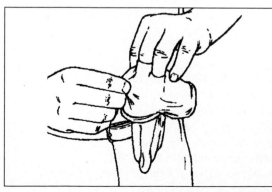

After removing both gloves ...

- Discard gloves in an appropriate container.
- Wash your hands thoroughly.

AMERICAN RED CROSS FIRST AID/CPR/AED PROGRAM

Examination A

Instructions:

Read each question slowly and carefully. Then choose the best answer. Fill in that circle on the answer sheet on page 23. When you are done with the examination, hand in the completed answer sheet to your instructor.

Section 1—Before Providing Care

1. The steps to follow in an emergency are—
   a) Check-Call-Care.
   b) Call-Check-Secure.
   c) Check-Care-Defibrillate.
   d) Early access-Early CPR-Early recognition.

2. How can you protect yourself from disease transmission when giving care?
   a) Avoid contacting the victim's blood or other body fluids.
   b) Ask the victim first if he or she has any communicable diseases.
   c) Use protective equipment, such as disposable gloves and breathing barriers, when giving care.
   d) A and C.

3. You come upon a scene where someone seems to be hurt. Why should you check the scene before approaching the victim?
   a) To find out what happened and how many victims there are
   b) To see if there are any bystanders who can help
   c) To ensure your own safety
   d) All of the above

4. You see someone on the ground in the parking lot who appears to be unconscious. After checking the scene for safety, what should you do next?
   a) Move the victim.
   b) Check the victim by gently tapping him and shouting; "Are you O.K?"
   c) Give CPR.
   d) Check for a pulse.

5. You see a co-worker collapse. You check the scene and then check the victim for consciousness, but she does not respond. What should you do next?

   a) [call emergency number.]
   b) Give 2 rescue breaths.
   c) Check for a pulse.
   d) Move the victim.

6. You and a co-worker enter the lunchroom and find a person lying on the floor. You check the scene and then you check the victim. Your co-worker is getting ready to move the victim onto a nearby sofa "to be more comfortable," and asks for your help. What should you do next?
   a) Help your co-worker move the victim.
   b) Start rescue breathing.
   c) Tell your co-worker not to move the victim since there is no immediate danger and moving the victim could cause further injury.
   d) Give the victim lots of water.

7. You respond to an emergency and find four victims. Which victim should you care for first?
   a) A victim who is bleeding lightly from his thigh
   b) A victim who is complaining of abdominal cramps
   c) A victim who has a burn on his forearm
   d) A victim who is unconscious

8. A person was injured when a heavy object fell on him in the warehouse. You think he may be in shock. Which of the following signals indicate the victim may be in shock?
   a) Restlessness and irritability
   b) Pale or ashen, cool, moist skin
   c) Nausea and vomiting
   d) All of the above

9. You determine that a victim is in shock. Which of the following should you **NOT** do for someone in shock?
   a) Keep the victim comfortable.
   b) Give the victim water.
   c) Monitor the victim's ABCs.
   d) Raise the victim's legs 12 inches.

10. A co-worker has been injured and is conscious. You should—

    b) Ask her to walk with you to the first aid station.
    c) Check her for life-threatening conditions and for conditions that may become life threatening.
    d) A and C.

Section 2—Adult CPR

1. You are in the cafeteria when a co-worker at the next table suddenly clutches his throat with both hands. You ask him if he is choking and he frantically nods yes. You tell him you are trained in first aid and that you can help. As you send someone to call 9-1-1, what should you do?

a) Try to give 2 slow breaths to the victim.
b) Check his carotid pulse, and then give back blows.
c) Give 15 chest compressions.
d) Stand behind the victim, and give abdominal thrusts.

2. You and a co-worker find someone on the floor unconscious. You send your co-worker to call 9-1-1. When you check the victim's breathing and pulse, you find that he is not breathing but has a pulse.

   You should—

a) Give quick breaths at the rate of 60 to 80 a minute.
b) Give CPR.
c) Give back blows and chest thrusts.
d) Breathe slowly into the victim about once every 5 seconds.

3. If your first 2 breaths do not go in during your care for an unconscious victim, what should you do next?

a) Reposition the victim's airway and reattempt 2 rescue breaths.
b) Give up to 5 abdominal thrusts.
c) Sweep out the mouth.
d) None of the above.

4. Where should you position your hands to give abdominal thrusts for a conscious choking victim?

a) On the rib cage
b) On the belly button
c) In the middle of the abdomen just above the belly button
d) Any of the above

5. To check if a victim is breathing—

a) Check for a pulse in the neck.
b) Look, listen, and feel for breathing.
c) Look in the victim's mouth for at least 10 seconds.
d) Hold your hands over the ribs to feel for chest expansion.

6. You notice that a co-worker looks uncomfortable. He is sweating and seems to be having trouble breathing. You ask him if he feels okay, and he says no, that he feels a heavy pressure in his chest. What life-threatening condition could he be experiencing?

a) Indigestion
b) Heart attack
c) Upset stomach
d) All of the above

7. You are called to help a co-worker who is not breathing and has no pulse. Why is it crucial for you to start CPR as quickly as possible?

a) CPR helps prevent a heart attack.
b) With early CPR, the victim will not need advanced medical care.
c) CPR helps circulate blood that contains oxygen to the vital organs until more advanced medical personnel arrive.
d) CPR helps restart a heart.

8. How long should you check a victim's pulse?

a) No more than 10 seconds
b) 1 to 3 seconds
c) About 60 seconds
d) About 15 to 20 seconds

9. Where should you place your hands to give chest compressions during CPR?

a) One hand on the notch and one hand on the ribs
b) On the center of the breastbone, just above the notch where the ribs meet the breastbone
c) On the left side of the rib cage, $3^1/_2$ inches from the breastbone
d) Over the abdomen, about 2 inches below where the ribs meet the breastbone

10. When giving CPR—

a) Compress the chest straight down about 2 inches.
b) Give cycles of 15 compressions and 2 slow breaths.
c) Compress the chest about $^1/_2$ inch.
d) A and B.

Section 3—First Aid

1. A co-worker has fallen to the ground and has been shaking uncontrollably for at least 5 minutes. Which of the following is most appropriate to care for this victim?
   a) Clear the area of objects that may injure the co-worker and have someone call 9-1-1 or the workplace emergency number.
   b) Try to prevent the victim from swallowing his tongue by placing your fingers in his mouth.
   c) Try to give the victim some sugar.
   d) Hold the victim down.

2. On the way to a meeting, a co-worker collapses in front of you. When she regains consciousness, she has difficulty speaking and one side of her face and body appear to be paralyzed. These signals lead you to believe your co-worker has—
   a) Had a stroke.
   b) Had a diabetic emergency.
   c) Had a seizure.
   d) Been poisoned.

3. You have bandaged a co-worker's cut forearm in a way that applies pressure on the wound and a co-worker has called 9-1-1. Blood is still soaking through the dressing and bandage. You help the man elevate his arm in an attempt to stop the bleeding, but the bleeding continues. What should you do now?
   a) Remove the dressing and bandage and start over again with a tighter bandage.
   b) Apply a tourniquet around the arm above the wound.
   c) Apply additional dressings and bandages, and apply pressure on the inside of the arm midway between the shoulder and elbow.
   d) Go to the doctor because there is nothing else you can do.

4. A co-worker burned her hand in the office lunchroom when she touched a stove burner she did not realize was hot. There are burns with blisters across the palm and several fingers. You are present in the room when this happens. What care should you give first?
   a) Cool the burn with large amounts of cool water.
   b) Cover the burn with a dry, sterile dressing.
   c) Blow on the burn to cool it off, or have her wave her hand around in the air.
   d) Apply some ointment or grease to the burn.

5. Your co-worker is bleeding severely. After putting on disposable gloves, what is the first step in your care?
   a) Press firmly against the wound with a sterile dressing.
   b) Apply pressure at a pressure point.
   c) Elevate the wound if there are no broken bones and you can do so without causing further pain.
   d) Let the wound bleed until it stops on its own.

6. A co-worker has injured his ankle in the warehouse. It seems to be a sprain, and another co-worker wants to drive him to a nearby clinic to have it examined by a doctor. You should immobilize the ankle—
   a) Because movement during transport could cause more injury.
   b) After it is examined by the doctor.
   c) Only if you can do so without causing more pain and discomfort to the victim.
   d) A and C.

7. The sling that you apply to an injured co-worker's arm should be—
   a) Loose, so that the victim can move the arm around.
   b) Snug, but not so tight that it slows circulation.
   c) Tied off directly over the injured area.
   d) None of the above.

8. It is a hot summer day, and you have been working outside. You think a co-worker may be suffering from heat exhaustion because he is sweating profusely and looks pale. Your care should include—
   a) Having the victim take a salt tablet.
   b) Rapidly transporting the victim to a medical facility.
   c) Removing him from the heat and giving him cool water to drink if he is conscious.
   d) Vigorously massaging the victim.

9. What care should you give to a co-worker with frost-bitten hands?
   a) Immerse his hands in hot water.
   b) Massage his hands vigorously.
   c) Have the victim shake his hands vigorously until feeling is restored.
   d) Rewarm the hands in warm water.

10. You begin to care for a victim of a heat-related emergency, but she becomes unconscious. What should you do first?
    a) Be sure 9-1-1 or the workplace emergency number has been called.
    b) Monitor the victim's airway.
    c) Give the victim ice to eat.
    d) Pour water on her face to try to revive her.

Section 4—Automated External Defibrillation

1. Early defibrillation is an important link in the cardiac chain of survival because—
a) Each minute that defibrillation is delayed reduces the chance of survival.
b) Defibrillation can help prevent stroke.
c) A cardiac arrest victim may have an unshockable rhythm.
d) All of the above.

2. Where should you attach the AED pads to the victim?
a) Place one pad on the center of the chest and the other pad on the victim's lower abdomen.
b) Place one pad on the victim's lower left side and the other pad on the victim's lower right side.
c) Place one pad on the victim's upper right chest and the other pad on the victim's lower left side.
d) Place both pads on the victim's upper chest.

3. Which of the following precautions apply when operating an AED?
a) Do not touch the victim while the AED is analyzing.
b) Do not touch the victim when defibrillating.
c) Do not use an AED on a victim lying in water.
d) All of the above.

4. Before delivering a shock with an AED, you should—
a) Do a finger sweep.
b) Place the victim on his or her side.
c) Have another responder hold the victim.
d) Instruct others to stand clear.

5. You are giving care to a victim with no pulse. After you give 2 shocks, the AED prompts, "No shock advised." What action should you take next?
a) Check for a pulse.
b) Push the shock button anyway.
c) Start CPR.
d) Give 2 slow breaths.

AMERICAN RED CROSS FIRST AID/CPR/AED PROGRAM

Examination B

Instructions:

Read each question slowly and carefully. Then choose the best answer.
Fill in that circle on the answer sheet on page 25. When you are done
with the examination, hand in the completed answer sheet to your instructor.

Section 1—Before Providing Care

1. How can you protect yourself from disease transmission when giving care?
   a) Avoid contacting the victim's blood or other body fluids.
   b) Ask the victim first if he or she has any communicable diseases.
   c) Use protective equipment, such as disposable gloves and breathing barriers, when giving care.
   d) A and C.

2. The steps to follow in an emergency are—
   a) Check-Call-Care.
   b) Call-Check-Secure.
   c) Check-Care-Defibrillate.
   d) Early access-Early CPR-Early recognition.

3. There is a commotion in your work area. One of your co-workers has fallen from a ladder. Your other co-workers are getting ready to move the injured victim and ask for your help. What should you do?
   a) Help your co-workers move the victim.
   b) Start rescue breathing.
   c) Tell your co-workers not to move the victim since there is no immediate danger and moving the victim could cause further injury.
   d) Give the victim lots of water.

4. A co-worker has been injured and is conscious. You should—
   a) Talk to her to find out what happened.
   b) Ask her to walk with you to the first aid station.
   c) Check her for life-threatening conditions and for conditions that may become life threatening.
   d) A and C.

5. You are at work when you see what looks like a serious accident between two vehicles. Why should you check the scene before giving care?
   a) To find out what happened and how many victims there are
   b) To ensure your own safety
   c) To see if there are any bystanders who can help
   d) All of the above

6. You respond to an emergency and find four victims. Which victim should you care for first?
   a) A victim who is bleeding lightly from his thigh
   b) A victim who is complaining of pain in his knee
   c) A victim who has a burn on his forearm
   d) A victim who is unconscious

7. You are on your lunch break when you notice a co-worker who appears to be unconscious. After checking the scene, you check the victim for consciousness by—
   a) Rolling him onto his side and sweeping his mouth.
   b) Calling, or have a co-worker call, 9-1-1 or the workplace emergency number.
   c) Gently tapping him and shouting; "Are you O.K.!"
   d) Checking for a pulse.

8. You see a co-worker collapse. You check the scene and then check the victim for consciousness, but she does not respond. What should you do next?
   a) Call, or have a co-worker call, 9-1-1 or the workplace emergency number.
   b) Give 2 rescue breaths.
   c) Check for a pulse.
   d) Move the victim.

9. You are helping a co-worker who is cut and bleeding severely. You control the bleeding, but you think the victim may be in shock. What should you do?
   a) Make sure 9-1-1 or the workplace emergency number has been called.
   b) Keep the victim from getting chilled or overheated.
   c) Monitor and reassure the victim until advanced medical help arrives.
   d) All of the above.

10. You determine that this victim is in shock. Which of the following should you NOT do for someone in shock?
    a) Keep the victim comfortable.
    b) Give the victim water.
    c) Monitor the victim's ABCs.
    d) Raise the victim's legs 12 inches.

Not to be reproduced without permission.

Section 2—Adult CPR

1. What is the purpose of CPR?
a) CPR restarts the heart.
b) With CPR, the victim will not need advanced medical care.
c) CPR helps circulate blood that contains oxygen to the vital organs until more advanced medical personnel arrive.
d) CPR helps prevent a heart attack.

2. You notice that a co-worker looks uncomfortable. He is sweating and seems to be having trouble breathing. You ask him if he feels okay, and he says no, that he feels a heavy pressure in his chest. What life-threatening condition could he be experiencing?
a) Indigestion
b) Heart attack
c) Upset stomach
d) All of the above

3. You are in the cafeteria when a co-worker at the next table suddenly clutches his throat with both hands. You ask him if he is choking and he frantically nods yes. You tell him you are trained in first aid and that you can help. As you send some-one to call 9-1-1, what should you do?
a) Try to give 2 slow breaths to the victim.
b) Check his carotid pulse, and then give back blows.
c) Give 15 chest compressions.
d) Stand behind the victim and give abdominal thrusts.

4. How long should you check a victim's pulse?
a) No more than 10 seconds
b) 1 to 3 seconds
c) About 60 seconds
d) About 15 to 20 seconds

5. When giving rescue breaths to an adult—
a) Give quick breaths at the rate of 60 to 80 a minute.
b) Give about 15 compressions.
c) Give back blows and chest thrusts.
d) Breathe slowly into the victim, about once every 5 seconds.

6. When giving care to a victim who is conscious and has an obstructed airway, where should you position your hands to give abdominal thrusts?
a) On the rib cage
b) On the belly button
c) In the middle of the abdomen just above the belly button
d) Any of the above

7. If your first 2 breaths do not go in during your care for an unconscious victim, what should you do next?
a) Reposition the victim's airway and reattempt 2 slow breaths.
b) Give up to 5 abdominal thrusts.
c) Sweep out the mouth.
d) None of the above.

8. To check if a victim is breathing—
a) Check for a pulse in the neck.
b) Look, listen, and feel for breathing.
c) Look in the victim's mouth for at least 10 seconds.
d) Hold your hands over the ribs to feel for chest expansion.

9. When giving CPR—
a) Compress the chest straight down about 2 inches.
b) Give cycles of 15 compressions and 2 slow breaths.
c) Compress the chest at an angle about $1/_2$ inch.
d) A and B.

10. Where should you place your hands to give chest compressions during CPR?
a) One hand on the notch and one hand on the ribs.
b) On the center of the breastbone, just above the notch where the ribs meet the breastbone.
c) On the left side of the rib cage $3^1/_2$ inches from the center.
d) Over the abdomen, about 2 inches below where the ribs meet the breastbone.

Section 3—First Aid

1. A co-worker collapses. As she regains consciousness she has difficulty speaking and one side of her face and body appear to be paralyzed. These signals lead you to believe your co-worker has—
   a) Had a stroke.
   b) Had a diabetic emergency.
   c) Had a seizure.
   d) Been poisoned.

2. A co-worker has fallen to the ground and has been shaking uncontrollably for at least 5 minutes. Which of the following is most appropriate to care for this victim?
   a) Clear the area of objects that may injure the co-worker and have someone call 9-1-1 or the workplace emergency number.
   b) Try to prevent the victim from swallowing his tongue by placing your fingers in his mouth.
   c) Try to give the victim some sugar.
   d) Hold the victim down.

3. If someone has injured a muscle, bone, or joint and is unable to move or use the injured part—
   a) Call, or have someone else call, 9-1-1 or the workplace emergency number.
   b) Have the person try to walk it off.
   c) Try to apply a splint before advanced medical personnel arrive and take over.
   d) Slowly move the injured part around until it feels better.

4. A co-worker seems to have sprained his ankle in the warehouse. He can move the injured ankle, but he has decided to go to a nearby clinic to have it examined. Another co-worker wants to drive him to the clinic. You should immobilize the ankle—
   a) Because movement during transport could cause more injury.
   b) After it is examined by the doctor.
   c) Only if you can do so without causing more pain and discomfort to the victim.
   d) A and C.

5. What care should you give to a co-worker with frost-bitten hands?
   a) Immerse his hands in hot water.
   b) Massage his hands vigorously.
   c) Have the victim shake his hands vigorously until feeling is restored.
   d) Rewarm the hands in warm water.

6. You begin to care for a victim of a heat-related emergency, and she becomes unconscious. What should you do first?
   a) Be sure 9-1-1 or the workplace emergency number has been called.
   b) Monitor the victim's airway.
   c) Give the victim ice to eat.
   d) Pour water on her face to try to revive her.

7. It is a hot summer day, and you have been working outside. You think a co-worker may be suffering from heat exhaustion because he is sweating profusely and looks pale. Your care for this victim should include—
   a) Having the victim take a salt tablet.
   b) Rapidly transporting the victim to a medical facility.
   c) Removing him from the heat and giving him cool water to drink if he is conscious.
   d) Vigorously massaging the victim.

8. A co-worker has burned his hand on some hot metal. There are burns with blisters across the palm and several fingers. How should you care for this burn injury?
   a) Blow on the burn to cool it off, or have him wave his hand around in the air.
   b) Raise the victim's feet about 12 inches.
   c) Cool the burn with large amounts of cool water, and then cover the burn with a dry, sterile dressing.
   d) Apply some ointment or lotion on the burn.

9. You have bandaged a co-worker's cut forearm in a way that applies pressure on the wound and a co-worker has called 9-1-1. Blood is still soaking through the dressing and bandage. You help the man elevate his arm in an attempt to stop the bleeding, but the bleeding continues. What should you do?
   a) Remove the dressing and bandage and start over again with a tighter bandage.
   b) Apply a tourniquet around the arm above the wound.
   c) Apply additional dressings and bandages, and apply pressure on the inside of the arm midway between the shoulder and elbow.
   d) Go to the doctor because there is nothing else you can do.

10. Your co-worker is bleeding severely. After putting on disposable gloves, what is the first step in your care?
    a) Press firmly against the wound with a clean or sterile dressing.
    b) Apply pressure at a pressure point.
    c) Elevate the wound if no broken bones and without causing further pain.
    d) Let the wound bleed until it stops on its own.

Section 4—Automated External Defibrillation

1. Early defibrillation is an important link in the cardiac chain of survival because—
   a) Each minute that defibrillation is delayed reduces the victim's chance of survival.
   b) Defibrillation can help prevent stroke.
   c) A cardiac arrest victim may have an unshockable rhythm.
   d) All of the above.

2. Where should you attach the AED pads to the victim?
   a) Place one pad on the center of the chest and the other pad on the victim's lower abdomen.
   b) Place one pad on the victim's lower left side and the other pad on the victim's lower right side.
   c) Place one pad on the victim's upper right chest and the other pad on the victim's lower left side.
   d) Place both pads on the victim's upper chest.

3. Which of the following precautions apply when using an AED?
   a) Do not touch the victim while the AED is analyzing.
   b) Do not touch the victim when defibrillating.
   c) Do not use an AED on a victim lying in water.
   d) All of the above.

4. Before delivering a shock with an AED you should—
   a) Do a finger sweep.
   b) Place the victim on his or her side.
   c) Have another responder hold the victim.
   d) Instruct others to stand clear.

5. You are giving care to a victim with no pulse. After you give 2 shocks the AED prompts, "No shock advised." What action should you take next?
   a) Check for a pulse.
   b) Push the shock button anyway.
   c) Start CPR.
   d) Give 2 slow breaths.

Section 2: Adult CPR/AED

Adult CPR/AED Course Outline

Topic	Lecture	Standard First Aid Video	Adult CPR/AED Skills Card	Participant's Booklet
Introduction	x		x	page 35
Check-Call-Care	x		x	page 36
Conscious Choking	x	x	x	page 37
Checking an Unconscious Victim	x	x	x	pages 37-38
Rescue Breathing	x	x	x	page 39
Cardiac Chain of Survival	x	x		pages 40-41
CPR	x	x	x	pages 42-43
Unconscious Choking	x	x	x	page 44
Using an AED	x	x	x	pages 45-46
Skill Scenarios	x			
Written Examination and Closing	x			pages 47-58

Lecture Point 1

Check-Call-Care

- Check the scene, then check the victim.

- Call 9-1-1 or the workplace/local emergency number.

- Care for the life-threatening conditions that you find.

Lecture Point 2

Life-threatening Conditions

- Unconsciousness

- Persistent chest pain or discomfort

- Not breathing, or having trouble breathing

- No signs of circulation

- Severe bleeding

- Seizures that last more than 5 minutes, recur, result in injury, or occur in someone who is pregnant or diabetic.

Lecture Point 3

Conscious Choking

■ Before caring for a conscious victim, you must first get his or her permission. This is called informed consent.

■ Identify yourself and ask the victim if you can help.

■ Tell the victim your level of training and the care you are going to provide.

Lecture Point 4

Basic Precautions

■ Use protective equipment, such as disposable gloves and breathing barriers.

■ Wash your hands immediately after giving care, using soap and warm water.

■ Avoid direct contact with a victim's blood and body fluids.

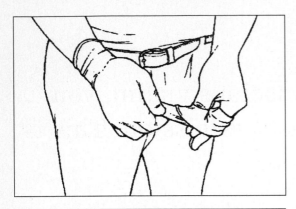

Partially remove first glove

- Pinch glove at the wrist, being careful to touch only the glove's outside surface.
- Pull glove toward the fingertips without completely removing it.
- The glove is now inside out.

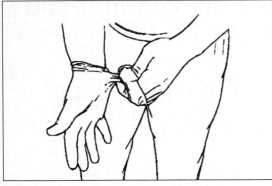

Remove second glove

- With partially gloved hand, pinch the exterior of second glove.

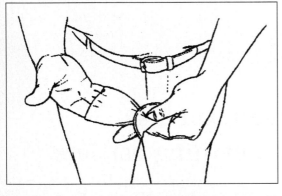

- Pull the second glove toward the fingertips until it is inside out, then remove it completely.

Finish removing both gloves

- Grasp both gloves with your free hand.
- Touch only the clean interior surface of the glove.

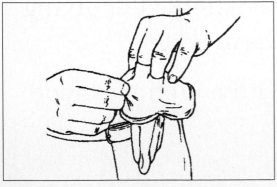

After removing both gloves ...

- Discard gloves in an appropriate container.
- Wash your hands thoroughly.

Lecture Point 5

Rescue Breathing

- A victim who is not breathing but shows signs of circulation needs rescue breathing.

- If a victim does not receive early care, he or she may go into cardiac arrest.

Lecture Point 6

Signals of a Heart Attack

- Persistent chest pain or discomfort lasting more than 3-5 minutes or that goes away and comes back

- Pain in either arm, discomfort or pressure that spreads to the shoulder, arm, neck, or jaw

- Nausea, shortness of breath, or trouble breathing

- Sweating, changes in skin appearance

- Dizziness or unconsciousness

Lecture Point 7

Cardiac Chain of Survival

- Early recognition and early access
- Early CPR
- Early defibrillation
- Early advanced life support

Lecture Point 8

CPR

- CPR helps circulate blood that contains oxygen to the vital organs.

- Do CPR by compressing the victim's chest and giving rescue breaths.

- A CPR cycle is 15 compressions and 2 rescue breaths.

- Four CPR cycles should take about 1 minute.

Lecture Point 9

Continue CPR—

- Until the scene becomes unsafe.

- Until you can see or feel signs of circulation.

- Until an AED is ready to use.

- You are too exhausted to continue.

- Another trained responder arrives and takes over.

Lecture Point 10

Unconscious Choking

■ If a person is unconscious, consent is implied. Implied consent means that the victim would agree to the care if he or she could.

■ If you give breaths to an unconscious victim and your breaths do not go in, reposition the airway by tilting the head further back and reattempt 2 rescue breaths.

■ If your breaths still do not go in, assume that the airway is blocked.

Lecture Point 11

AED

- An automated external defibrillator (AED) is a machine that analyzes the heart's rhythm and, if necessary, tells you to deliver a shock to a victim of sudden cardiac arrest.

- This shock, called defibrillation, may help the heart to reestablish an effective rhythm.

- If the AED tells you "No shock advised," check the victim's pulse.

Lecture Point 12

AED Precautions

- Do not touch the victim while the AED is analyzing or defibrillating.

- Do not use alcohol to wipe the victim's chest dry or use an AED around other flammable materials.

- Do not use an AED in a moving vehicle.

- Do not use an AED on a victim lying on a conductive surface or in water.

- Do not use an AED on a child under age 8 or under 55 pounds.

- Do not use an AED on a victim wearing a nitroglycerin patch or other patch on the chest. With a gloved hand, remove any patches from the chest before attaching the device.

- Do not use a cellular phone or radio transmitter within 6 feet of the AED.

Answer Sheet: American Red Cross Adult CPR/AED Written Examination

Ⓐ Ⓑ

Name _____   Date _____

DIRECTIONS

Beside the number of each question, fill in with a pencil the circle containing the letter of your answer. To pass the examination, you must score 80 percent or above.

You may wish to go back and check your answers to be sure that you matched the right answer with the right question.

---

1. (a) (b) (c) (d)   16. (a) (b) (c) (d)
2. (a) (b) (c) (d)   17. (a) (b) (c) (d)
3. (a) (b) (c) (d)   18. (a) (b) (c) (d)
4. (a) (b) (c) (d)   19. (a) (b) (c) (d)
5. (a) (b) (c) (d)   20. (a) (b) (c) (d)
6. (a) (b) (c) (d)   21. (a) (b) (c) (d)
7. (a) (b) (c) (d)   22. (a) (b) (c) (d)
8. (a) (b) (c) (d)   23. (a) (b) (c) (d)
9. (a) (b) (c) (d)   24. (a) (b) (c) (d)
10. (a) (b) (c) (d)   25. (a) (b) (c) (d)
11. (a) (b) (c) (d)
12. (a) (b) (c) (d)
13. (a) (b) (c) (d)
14. (a) (b) (c) (d)
15. (a) (b) (c) (d)

Answer Sheet: American Red Cross Adult CPR/AED Written Examination

(A) **(B)**

Name _____ Date _____

1.	(a)	(b)	(c)	(d)	16.	(a) (b) (c) (d)
2.	(a)	(b)	(c)	(d)	17.	(a) (b) (c) (d)
3.	(a)	(b)	(c)	(d)	18.	(a) (b) (c) (d)
4.	(a)	(b)	(c)	(d)	19.	(a) (b) (c) (d)
5.	(a)	(b)	(c)	(d)	20.	(a) (b) (c) (d)
6.	(a)	(b)	(c)	(d)	21.	(a) (b) (c) (d)
7.	(a)	(b)	(c)	(d)	22.	(a) (b) (c) (d)
8.	(a)	(b)	(c)	(d)	23.	(a) (b) (c) (d)
9.	(a)	(b)	(c)	(d)	24.	(a) (b) (c) (d)
10.	(a)	(b)	(c)	(d)	25.	(a) (b) (c) (d)
11.	(a)	(b)	(c)	(d)		
12.	(a)	(b)	(c)	(d)		
13.	(a)	(b)	(c)	(d)		
14.	(a)	(b)	(c)	(d)		
15.	(a)	(b)	(c)	(d)		

IMPORTANT: Read all instructions before beginning this examination.

INSTRUCTIONS: Mark all answers in pencil on a separate answer sheet. **Do not write on this examination.** The questions on this examination are multiple choice. Read each question slowly and carefully. Then choose the **best** answer and fill in that circle on the answer sheet. If you wish to change an answer, erase your first answer completely. Return this examination to your instructor when you are finished.

EXAMPLE

ANSWER SHEET

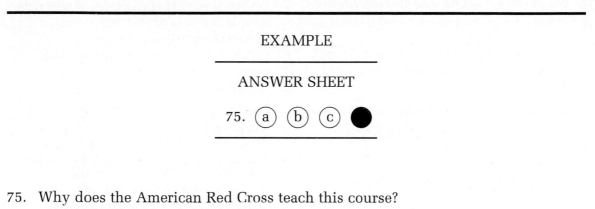

---

75. Why does the American Red Cross teach this course?
    a. To help people stay calm in emergencies
    b. To help people make appropriate decisions when they confront an emergency
    c. To help people in an emergency keep a victim's injuries from getting worse until EMS arrives
    d. All of the above

51

1. The three emergency action steps to follow in an emergency are—
a. Check the scene and the victim; call 9-1-1 or the workplace/local emergency number; care for the victim.
b. Call 9-1-1 or the workplace/local emergency number; check the victim; secure the scene.
c. Check the scene; look, listen, and feel for breathing; provide early defibrillation.
d. Provide early access, early CPR, and early defibrillation.

2. Why should you check the scene in an emergency?
a. To find out what happened and how many victims there are
b. For your own safety and for bystanders who can assist
c. To check if the victim is breathing and has a pulse
d. Both a and b

3. Which of the following is a life-threatening condition?
a. A person with persistent chest pain or discomfort
b. A person who has a sunburn
c. A person who is coughing forcefully
d. A person who is conscious and has a sprained ankle

4. You see a co-worker collapse. You check the scene and check the victim for consciousness but she does not respond. What should you do?
a. Call, or have a co-worker call, 9-1-1 or the workplace emergency number.
b. Give up to three shocks with the defibrillator.
c. Give abdominal thrusts.
d. Begin CPR immediately.

5. A person having a heart attack—
a. May have persistent chest pain or discomfort.
b. May be sweating and have trouble breathing.
c. Requires medical care at once.
d. All of the above.

6. To check if a person is unconscious—
a. Gently tap the person and shout, "Are you O.K?"
b. Check for any medical tags.
c. Try to breathe into the person.
d. Put the victim on his side in case he vomits.

7. Early CPR is an important link in the cardiac chain of survival because—
a. CPR helps prevent heart attacks.
b. With early CPR, most cardiac arrest victims do not need defibrillation.
c. CPR helps circulate blood that contains oxygen to the vital organs until an AED is used or advanced medical personnel arrive.
d. It helps restart the heart.

8. Early defibrillation is an important link in the cardiac chain of survival because—
a. Each minute that defibrillation is delayed reduces the chance of survival by about 10 percent.
b. Defibrillation can help prevent stroke.
c. A cardiac arrest victim may have an unshockable rhythm.
d. All of the above.

9. Where should you attach the AED pads to the victim?
a. Place one pad on the center of the chest and the other pad on the victim's lower abdomen.
b. Place one pad on the victim's lower left side and the other pad on the victim's lower right side.
c. Place one pad on the victim's upper right chest and the other pad on the victim's lower left side.
d. Place both pads on the victim's upper chest.

10. When preparing an AED for use, what is the first thing you should do?
a. Turn on the AED.
b. Deliver a shock.
c. Stand clear.
d. Begin $1^1/_2$ minutes of CPR.

11. Which of the following precautions apply when operating an AED?
a. Do not touch the victim while the AED is analyzing.
b. Do not touch the victim when defibrillating.
c. Do not use an AED on a victim lying in water.
d. All of the above.

12. Before delivering a shock with an AED you should—
a. Look for a foreign object in the victim's mouth.
b. Place the victim on his or her side.
c. Have another responder hold the victim.
d. Instruct others to stand clear.

13. Before using an AED you should—
a. Check that the victim shows no signs of circulation (pulse).
b. Give abdominal thrusts.
c. Move the victim to a semi-reclined position.
d. Take the victim's temperature.

14. When giving abdominal thrusts to a conscious choking adult—
a. Stand in front of the victim.
b. Check the carotid pulse; then give back blows.
c. Shout, shake, and then shock the victim.
d. Place your hands just above the victim's belly button and give quick, upward thrusts.

15. When giving chest compressions and breaths during CPR—
a. Compress the chest about 2 inches deep.
b. Give 2 rescue breaths.
c. Give cycles of 15 compressions and 2 rescue breaths.
d. All of the above.

16. The correct hand position for giving CPR is—
a. On the notch where the ribs meet the breastbone.
b. On the center of the breastbone, just above the notch where the ribs meet the breastbone.
c. On the left side of the rib cage $3^1/_2$ inches from the center.
d. None of the above.

17. A co-worker of yours has been electrocuted and shows no signs of circulation (pulse). What should you do before letting the AED analyze the heart rhythm?
a. Instruct others to stand clear.
b. Deliver a shock by pushing the shock button.
c. Give 1 rescue breath every 5 seconds.
d. Deliver 2 shocks.

18. You are giving care to a victim with no signs of circulation (pulse). After you give two shocks the AED prompts, "No shock advised." What action should you take next?
a. Check for a pulse.
b. Push the shock button anyway.
c. Start CPR.
d. Give 2 rescue breaths.

19. What care should you give a conscious adult who is choking and cannot cough, speak, or breathe?
a. Give 2 rescue breaths.
b. Look for a foreign object in the victim's mouth.
c. Give abdominal thrusts.
d. Lower the victim to the floor and open the airway.

20. To give rescue breathing to an adult—
a. Give quick breaths at the rate of 60 to 80 a minute.
b. Breathe slowly into the victim about once every 10 seconds.
c. Give rescue breaths rapidly about 3 times every 8 seconds.
d. Give 1 rescue breath every 5 seconds.

21. To check if a victim is breathing—
a. Check for a pulse in the neck.
b. Look, listen, and feel for breathing.
c. Look in the victim's mouth for at least 10 seconds.
d. Push the analyze button.

22. A victim who is not breathing but has signs of circulation (pulse)—
a. Has had a sudden cardiac arrest.
b. Needs compressions and breaths.
c. Needs rescue breathing.
d. Needs defibrillation.

23. For how many seconds do you check a victim's signs of circulation?
a. No more than 10 seconds
b. 3 to 5 seconds
c. About 60 seconds
d. About 15 to 20 seconds

24. Where should you position your hands when giving chest compressions to an unconscious choking adult?
a. On the rib cage.
b. On top of the notch at the lower end of the breastbone.
c. On the center of the breastbone, just above the notch where the ribs meet the breastbone.
d. Either A or B.

25. If your initial two breaths do not go in during your care for an unconscious adult, you should then—
a. Reposition the victim's head and reattempt 2 rescue breaths.
b. Give up to 5 abdominal thrusts.
c. Sweep out the mouth.
d. None of the above.

IMPORTANT: Read all instructions before beginning this examination.

INSTRUCTIONS: Mark all answers in pencil on a separate answer sheet. **Do not write on this examination.** The questions on this examination are multiple choice. Read each question slowly and carefully. Then choose the **best** answer and fill in that circle on the answer sheet. If you wish to change an answer, erase your first answer completely. Return this examination to your instructor when you are finished.

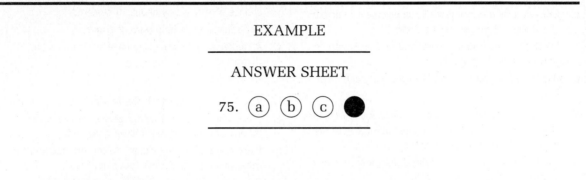

EXAMPLE

ANSWER SHEET

75. ⓐ ⓑ ⓒ ●

---

75. Why does the American Red Cross teach this course?
   a. To help people stay calm in emergencies
   b. To help people make appropriate decisions when they confront an emergency
   c. To help people in an emergency keep a victim's injuries from getting worse until EMS arrives
   d. All of the above

---

1. Why should you check the scene in an emergency?
a. To find out what happened and how many victims there are
b. For your own safety and for bystanders who can assist
c. To check if the victim is breathing and shows signs of circulation.
d. Both A and B

2. The three emergency action steps to follow in an emergency are—
a. Check the scene and the victim; call 9-1-1 or the workplace/local emergency number; care for the victim.
b. Call 9-1-1 or the workplace/local emergency number; check the victim; secure the scene.
c. Check the scene; look, listen, and feel for breathing; provide early defibrillation.
d. Provide early access, early CPR, and early defibrillation.

3. You see a co-worker collapse. You check the scene and check the victim for consciousness but she does not respond. What should you do?
a. Call 9-1-1 or the workplace/local emergency number, or have another co-worker call.
b. Give up to three shocks with the defibrillator.
c. Give abdominal thrusts.
d. Begin CPR immediately.

4. Which of the following is a life-threatening condition?
a. A person with persistent chest pain or discomfort
b. A person who has a sunburn
c. A person who is coughing forcefully
d. A person who is conscious and has a sprained ankle

5. A person having a heart attack—
a. May have persistent chest pain or discomfort.
b. May be sweating and have trouble breathing.
c. Requires medical care at once.
d. All of the above.

6. To check if a person is unconscious—
a. Gently tap the person and shout, "Are you O.K?"
b. Check for any medical tags.
c. Try to breathe into the person.
d. Put the victim on his side in case he vomits.

7. Early CPR is an important link in the cardiac chain of survival because—
a. CPR helps prevent heart attacks.
b. With early CPR, most cardiac arrest victims do not need defibrillation.
c. CPR helps circulate blood that contains oxygen to the vital organs until an AED is used or advanced medical personnel arrive.
d. It helps restart the heart.

8. Early defibrillation is an important link in the cardiac chain of survival because—
a. Each minute that defibrillation is delayed reduces the chance of survival by about 10 percent.
b. Defibrillation can help prevent stroke.
c. A cardiac arrest victim may have an unshockable rhythm.
d. All of the above.

9. Where should you attach the AED pads to the victim?
a. Place one pad on the center of the chest and the other pad on the victim's lower abdomen.
b. Place one pad on the victim's lower left side and the other pad on the victim's lower right side.
c. Place one pad on the victim's upper right chest and the other pad on the victim's lower left side.
d. Place both pads on the victim's upper chest.

10. Which of the following precautions apply when operating an AED?
a. Do not touch the victim while the AED is analyzing.
b. Do not touch the victim when defibrillating.
c. Do not use an AED on a victim lying in water.
d. All of the above.

11. When preparing an AED for use, what is the first thing you should do?
a. Turn on the AED.
b. Deliver a shock.
c. Stand clear.
d. Begin $1^1/_2$ minutes of CPR.

12. Before delivering a shock with an AED you should—
a. Look for a foreign object in the victim's mouth.
b. Place the victim on his or her side.
c. Have another responder hold the victim.
d. Instruct others to stand clear.

13. Before using an AED you should—
a. Check that the victim shows no signs of circulation (pulse).
b. Give abdominal thrusts.
c. Move the victim to a semi-reclined position.
d. Take the victim's temperature.

14. When giving abdominal thrusts to a conscious choking victim—
a. Stand in front of the victim.
b. Check the carotid pulse, then give back blows.
c. Shout, shake, and then shock the victim.
d. Place your hands just above the victim's belly button and give quick, upward thrusts.

15. When giving chest compressions and breaths during CPR—
a. Compress the chest about 2 inches deep.
b. Give 2 rescue breaths.
c. Give cycles of 15 compressions and 2 rescue breaths.
d. All of the above.

16. A co-worker of yours has been electrocuted and has no signs of circulation (pulse). What should you do before letting the AED analyze the heart rhythm?
a. Instruct others to stand clear.
b. Deliver a shock by pushing the shock button.
c. Give 1 rescue breath every 5 seconds.
d. Deliver 2 shocks.

17. The correct hand position for giving CPR is—
a. On the notch where the ribs meet the breastbone.
b. On the center of the breastbone, just above the notch where the ribs meet the breastbone.
c. On the left side of the rib cage $3^1/_2$ inches from the center.
d. None of the above.

18. You are giving care to a victim with no signs of circulation (pulse). After you give two shocks the AED prompts, "No shock advised." What action should you take next?
a. Check for a pulse.
b. Push the shock button anyway.
c. Start CPR.
d. Give 2 rescue breaths.

19. What care should you give a conscious adult who is choking and cannot cough, speak, or breathe?
a. Give 2 rescue breaths.
b. Look for a foreign object in the victim's mouth.
c. Give abdominal thrusts.
d. Lower the victim to the floor and open the airway.

20. To give rescue breaths to an adult—
a. Give quick breaths at the rate of 60 to 80 a minute.
b. Give 15 compressions and 2 breaths.
c. Breathe once every 8 seconds.
d. Give rescue breaths slowly into the victim about once every 5 seconds.

21. To check if a victim is breathing—
a. Check for a pulse in the neck.
b. Look, listen, and feel for breathing for about 5 seconds.
c. Look in the victim's mouth for at least 10 seconds.
d. Push the analyze button.

22. For how many seconds do you check the pulse of an adult?
a. No more than 10 seconds
b. 3 to 5 seconds
c. About 60 seconds
d. About 15 to 20 seconds

23. A victim who is not breathing but shows signs of circulation—
a. Has had a sudden cardiac arrest.
b. Needs compressions and breaths.
c. Needs rescue breathing.
d. Needs defibrillation.

24. To care for an unconscious choking adult—
a. Attempt to give 2 rescue breaths.
b. Give 15 chest compressions.
c. Look for a foreign object in the victim's mouth.
d. All of the above.

25. Where do you position your hands when giving chest compressions to an unconscious choking adult?
a. On the rib cage
b. On top of the notch at the lower end of the breast-bone
c. On the center of the breastbone, just above the notch where the ribs meet the breastbone
d. Either A or B

Section 3: Infant & Child CPR

Child CPR Course Outline

Topic	Lecture	Infant & Child Video	Infant & Child CPR Skills Card	Participant's Booklet
Introduction	x	x	x	pages 59, 61-66
Recognizing Emergencies	x			
Protecting Yourself	x			page 67
Before Providing Care	x		x	page 68
Conscious Choking—Child	x	x	x	
Prioritizing Care—Child	x	x	x	pages 68-69
Rescue Breathing—Child	x	x	x	
Cardiac Emergencies/ Unconscious Choking—Child	x	x	x	
Review—Child			x	
Written Examination and Closing—Child	x			pages 71-80

Infant CPR Course Outline

Topic	Lecture	Infant & Child Video	Infant & Child CPR Skills Card	Participant's Booklet
Introduction	x	x	x	pages 59, 61-66
Recognizing Emergencies	x			
Protecting Yourself	x			page 67
Before Providing Care	x		x	page 68
Prioritizing Care—Infant	x	x	x	page 69
Breathing Emergencies—Infant	x	x	x	
Cardiac Emergencies/ Unconscious Choking—Infant	x	x	x	
Review—Infant			x	
Written Examination and Closing—Infant	x			pages 71-80

Infant and Child CPR Course Outline

Topic	Lecture	Infant & Child Video	Infant & Child CPR Skills Card	Participant's Booklet
Introduction	x	x	x	pages 60-66
Recognizing Emergencies	x			
Protecting Yourself	x			page 67
Before Providing Care	x		x	page 68
Conscious Choking—Child	x	x	x	
Prioritizing Care—Child	x	x	x	page 70
Rescue Breathing—Child	x	x	x	
Cardiac Emergencies/ Unconscious Choking—Child	x	x	x	
Review—Child			x	
Prioritizing Care—Infant	x	x	x	
Breathing Emergencies—Infant	x	x	x	
Cardiac Emergencies/ Unconscious Choking—Infant	x	x	x	
Review—Infant			x	
Written Examination and Closing—Infant and Child	x	x	x	pages 71-80

"CHECK IT OUT!"
Safety Checklist

General Precautions

❏ Stairways and hallways are kept uncluttered and well lit. Safety gates are installed at all open stairways.

❏ Child guards are installed around fireplaces, wood-burning stoves, space heaters, radiators, and hot pipes.

❏ Curtain cords and shade pulls are kept out of children's reach.

❏ Plastic bags are kept out of the reach of children and pets.

❏ Fire extinguishers, first aid kits, and flashlights are installed in areas where they might be needed.

❏ A planned emergency escape route with meeting location is in place and practiced.

❏ The hot water temperature is set below 120° F to prevent accidental scalding.

❏ Knives, guns, ammunition, power tools, razor blades, scissors, and other objects that can cause injury are stored in locked cabinets or storage areas.

❏ Purses, handbags, brief cases, etc., including those of visitors, are kept out of children's reach.

❏ A list of emergency phone numbers and medications taken (and by whom) is posted near telephones.

❏ Windows and balcony doors have childproof latches.

❏ Balconies have protective barriers to prevent children from slipping through bars.

❏ Loose electrical cords are out of the flow of traffic. Multicord or octopus plugs (which can overheat) are not used.

❏ Smoke detectors are installed on each floor and especially near sleeping areas. Batteries are changed yearly.

❏ Space heaters are placed out of the reach of children and away from curtains.

❏ Flammable liquids, medicines, pesticides, and other toxic materials are securely stored in their original containers and locked out of the reach of children.

❏ The toy box has ventilation holes, a sliding door or panel, and a lightweight lid or a hinged lid with a support to hold it open in any position to which it is raised.

❏ The crib mattress has a firm, flat, tight-fitting mattress and all soft bedding and pillow-like items have been removed from the crib before putting the infant down to sleep (to prevent suffocation).

❏ Swimming pools and hot tubs are completely enclosed with a barrier (i.e., a locked fence and locked safety cover, respectively), and young children are kept away from them unless there is constant adult supervision.

Bathroom

❏ The bathroom door is kept closed.

❏ ALWAYS supervise children when they are around water (tub, basin, toilet) and/or electricity.

❏ Medicines and cleaning products are in containers with safety caps and locked away in cabinets with safety latches.

❏ Hair dryers and other appliances are stored away from sinks, tubs, and toilets.

❏ The bottom of the tub/shower has non-slip surfacing.

Kitchen

❏ Small appliances are kept unplugged when not in use and stored out of reach of children.

❏ Hot liquids and foods are handled with easily available potholders. Use the stove's back burners and keep pot handles turned to the back of the stove.

❏ Highchairs are placed away from the stove and other hot objects. Don't leave an infant alone in a highchair; always use all safety straps.

❏ Stove and sink areas are well-lit and there is ample countertop space.

❏ The kitchen is equipped with a stepladder or step stool so you do not have to use a chair to reach overhead objects.

Outside the Home/Play Area

❏ Trash is kept in tightly covered containers.

❏ Sandboxes are covered when not in use.

❏ Seatbelts and properly attached car seats are used for all trips in the car (truck, van, etc.).

For product safety information, call the U.S. Consumer Product Safety Commission's toll-free "Consumer Hotline" at 1-800-638-2772. Hearing- and speech-impaired callers can dial 1-800-638-8270. Or, visit their website at www.cpsc.gov

SAFETY PREVENTION TIPS

CHILD PASSENGER SAFETY

Using car safety seats and vehicle restraints properly is very important for infants and children. Safety restraints, properly used, help prevent death and injury. Follow these guidelines to make sure all infants and children are safe passengers.

- The best car safety seat—
  - Fits in the vehicle appropriately.
  - Fits the child properly.
  - Is used correctly.
  - Has never been in a crash.

- The infant's car seat should face the rear of the vehicle until the infant is at least 20 pounds AND 1 year of age.
- Infants who weigh 20 pounds before age 1 should ride facing the rear in a convertible seat or infant seat approved for higher weights until 1 year of age.
- A rear-facing car safety seat must NEVER be placed in the front passenger seat. Assume that all vehicles have air bags, which are dangerous to children and infants in the front seat.
- In rear-facing car safety seats for infants, shoulder straps must be at **or below** the infant's shoulders. The harness must be snug, and the car safety seat retainer clip should be positioned at the midpoint of the infant's chest, not at the abdomen or the neck.
- A belt-positioning booster seat should be used when the child has outgrown a convertible safety seat but is too small to fit properly in a vehicle safety belt.
- When the vehicle safety belt fits properly, the lap belt lies low and tight across the child's hips (not the abdomen) and the shoulder belt lies flat across the shoulder, away from the neck and face. Usually a child weighing 80 pounds and 5 feet in height can fit appropriately in a vehicle safety belt.

CHOKING PREVENTION FOR INFANTS AND CHILDREN

Dangerous Foods

Do not feed children younger than 4 years old any round, firm food unless it is chopped completely.

The following foods can be choking hazards:
- Hot dogs
- Nuts
- Chunks of meat or cheese
- Hard or sticky candy
- Popcorn
- Raw carrots
- Whole grapes
- Chunks of peanut butter

Dangerous Household Items

Keep the following household items stored safely out of reach of infants and children:
- Balloons
- Coins
- Marbles
- Small toy parts
- Pen or marker caps
- Small button-type batteries
- Small compressible toys that can fit entirely into a child's mouth
- Plastic bags

Action Steps to Prevent Choking

- Seat children in a high chair or at a table while they eat.
- Do not let children eat too fast.
- Give infants soft food that they do not need to chew.
- Supervise children while they eat.
- Cut food into small bites for infants and young children, and teach them to chew their food well.

FIRE SAFETY TIPS

If a fire occurs, would you know what to do? Follow these safety guidelines to protect those you care about.

Install and Maintain Smoke Detectors

- Smoke detectors save lives by giving you more time to escape safely. Install them on every level of your home, especially near sleeping areas.
- Test and vacuum detectors monthly. (Dust can impair their effectiveness.)
- Replace smoke detector batteries when you change your clocks in the spring and fall.

Plan and Practice an Escape Plan

- Plan two ways out of every room (not including elevators).
- Choose a meeting place outside where everyone should gather in case of a fire.
- Practice your plan every month to make sure everyone knows what to do.

Learn How to Use a Fire Extinguisher

- Place fire extinguishers at every level of your home, especially in the kitchen, basement, and garage. These areas have the greatest danger of a chemical or electrical fire.
- Practice how to use the fire extinguisher.
- Check them monthly to make sure they are in proper working condition by following the manufacturer's guidelines.

Make Sure Your Address is Visible

- Make sure your house or business number is visible from the street in a well-lit area so it can be seen at night, and the fire department can easily find you, if necessary.
- Check with your local fire department if you need an address sign made for you.

Use Electrical Appliances Safely

- Check lamps and ceiling fixtures to make sure wiring is intact.
- If an appliance smokes or smells, unplug or turn it off immediately.
- Examine electrical cords before use and replace any that are frayed or cracked.
- Do not overload electrical outlets.
- Use safety plugs to prevent electrical fires.

If a Fire Does Occur—

- If you must get through smoke to escape, keep low to the floor.
- The cleanest air will be 12 to 14 inches above the floor.
- Crawl on your hands and knees to get to the nearest safe exit.
- If possible, cover your mouth and nose with a damp cloth or handkerchief.
- IN A FIRE NEVER GO BACK INSIDE OF THE HOUSE TO GET ANYTHING.

Don't Play with Fire

- Teach children that matches and lighters are not toys and are dangerous.
- Store lighters and matches where a child cannot get to them.
- Keep burning candles away from infants and children.

PLAYGROUND SAFETY

Make it a top priority to keep children's play areas safe.

Supervision is Always a Must!

- Adult supervision is always needed on the playground.
  - Watch for potential hazards and keep areas free of glass, sharp items, and other dangerous items.
  - Observe children playing, and intervene and assist play when necessary.
  - Children should avoid wearing clothing with drawstrings around the neck.

Age Matters for Safe Play

- Preschoolers, ages 2-5, and children, ages 5-12, need separate play areas and different equipment.

Soften the Possible Falls

- Most playground injuries are caused by falls.
- The playground surface should contain material that meets or exceeds the critical height requirement as identified by the U.S. Consumer Product Safety Commission (http://www.cpsc.gov). Check with the manufacturer/supplier and the governing body of your area. Below are some examples of some common materials:
  - Wood Chips/Engineered Wood Fibers
  - Mulch
  - Gravel
  - Sand
  - Synthetic Materials—
    - Poured-in-Place
    - Rubber Mats

Equipment Safety

- Equipment needs to be anchored safely in the ground.
- All equipment pieces should be in good working order.
  - S-hooks are completely closed.
  - Bolts are not protruding.
  - There are no exposed footings.

POISON PREVENTION

Poison-proof any area where children or infants may be present.
- Close any container of a substance that could harm a child or infant as soon as you have finished using it.
- Keep pills in their original container.
- Keep all medicines, iron-containing vitamins, and household cleaning products out of reach and out of sight of children.
- Never keep medicines on a countertop or bedside table.
- Follow medicine label directions carefully to avoid accidental overdoses or misdoses that could result in accidental poisoning.
- Keep containers that use cake deodorizers (such as diaper pails) securely closed.
- Keep poisonous plants out of children's reach.
- Never refer to medicine as candy.

Poison Control Center Number (found in the front of the phone book) _____

65

SUN EXPOSURE

To prevent sunburn and other health problems, protect infants and children from the sun. Help children learn good habits for their future years.

- Schedule outdoor activities before 10 a.m. and after 3 p.m. (standard time) or before 11 a.m. and after 4 p.m. (daylight savings time).
- Monitor the daily UV Index forecasts for your area (at www.epa.gov, television, or in newspapers) and plan indoor activities on days of high sun intensity.
- Teach children how to find good shade areas.
- Keep infants and small children in the shade outdoors.
- Plan trips to parks and places where adequate shade is available.
- Plant shade trees on school or child care center property.
- Use portable shade structures, such as umbrellas, tents, and tarps.
- Build permanent shade structures, such as porches, picnic shelters, and fabric shade canopies.
- Include shade coverings in the design of playground equipment and recreational areas.
- Use a sunscreen with a sun protection factor (SPF) of at least 15 that blocks both UVA and UVB rays.
- Use broad-brimmed hats to shade the infant's or child's head, face, scalp, ears, and neck from the sun.
- Use sunglasses to protect the infant's or child's eyes. Excessive sun exposure can cause cataracts later in life.

WATER SAFETY TIPS

Take steps to keep little ones safe while they enjoy the water. These water safety tips help you and your children stay safe in, on, and around the water.

- Learn to swim.
  - The American Red Cross has swimming courses for people of any age and swimming ability. Contact your local Red Cross about available classes.
- Always swim with a buddy; never swim alone.
- Swim only in supervised areas.
- Obey all rules, signs, and lifeguard instructions.
- Watch out for the "dangerous too's"—
  - Too tired.
  - Too cold.
  - Too far from safety.
  - Too much sun.
  - Too much strenuous activity.
- Don't mix alcohol and swimming.
  - Alcohol impairs your judgment, balance, and coordination, affects your swimming and diving skills, and reduces your body's ability to stay warm. It also reduces your ability to supervise infants and children.
- Pay attention to local weather conditions and forecasts.
  - Stop swimming at the first indication of bad weather.
- Know how to prevent, recognize, and respond to water emergencies.
- Always model safe behavior.

66

Removing Disposable Gloves

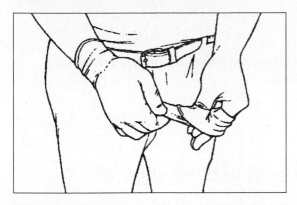

Partially remove first glove

- Pinch glove at the wrist, being careful to touch only the glove's outside surface.
- Pull glove toward the fingertips without completely removing it.
- The glove is now inside out.

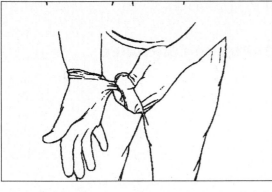

Remove second glove

- With partially gloved hand, pinch the exterior of second glove.

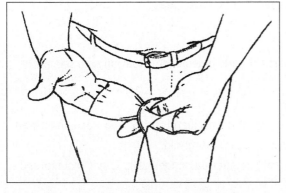

- Pull the second glove toward the fingertips until it is inside out, then remove it completely.

Finish removing both gloves

- Grasp both gloves with your free hand.
- Touch only the clean interior surface of the glove.

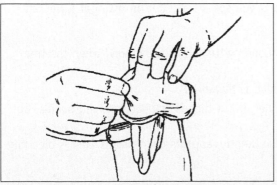

After removing both gloves ...

- Discard gloves in an appropriate container.
- Wash your hands thoroughly.

BEFORE PROVIDING CARE—INFANT AND CHILD

When to Call 9-1-1 Quiz

Directions:

Place a checkmark in the box next to any life-threatening conditions in which 9-1-1 or the workplace (local) emergency number should be called:

❏ **Minor bruise on the arm**

❏ **A cat scratch on the cheek**

❏ **Girl found at the bottom of a pool with no signs of circulation**

❏ **Not breathing**

❏ **Bleeding from the knee that cannot be controlled**

❏ **Deep burn on the face**

PRIORITIZING CARE—CHILD

Prioritizing Care Activity

In an emergency with more than one victim, you may need to prioritize care **(determine who needs help first).**

Directions:

Read the following emergency situations. Circle the victim in each emergency situation who has a life-threatening condition and needs help first.

Emergency Situation—1

You are the first person to stop on a busy highway to assist at an accident scene. Who needs help first?

Victim 1 The driver who is calling for help but otherwise appears uninjured.

Victim 2 An infant, who is seated in a car seat in the back middle passenger seat, is not moving and appears to be unconscious.

Victim 3 The older child behind the mother is crying and you see a small cut on his right lower leg.

Emergency Situation—2

Three children playing in a tree house in the backyard suddenly tumble to the ground when the tree house falls to one side. Who needs help first?

Victim 1 The child who has a gash on his forehead, which is bleeding.

Victim 2 The child who is crying and trying to remove her arm, which is trapped between boards, but does not appear to be bleeding.

Victim 3 The child who was hit by falling boards is lying quietly, appears unconscious, and is bleeding from a gash on his arm.

68

Emergency Situation—3

You go to a cafeteria for lunch. You see a young mother feeding her children when you hear a crash. Who needs help first?

Victim 1 The crying toddler who fell from her high chair.

Victim 2 The school-aged child who looks panicked and is clutching his throat.

Victim 3 The mother, who is bleeding from her hand.

PRIORITIZING CARE—INFANT

Prioritizing Care Activity

In an emergency with more than one victim, you may need to prioritize care **(determine who needs help first).**

Directions:

Read the following emergency situations. Circle the victim in each emergency situation who has a life-threatening condition and needs help first.

Emergency Situation—1

You are at a friend's home having coffee. Your friend is babysitting a 7-month-old infant. Your friend's children, ages 4 and 6, are quietly playing with the infant in the living room. You suddenly hear a crash and the older children screaming. Dashing into the room, you find several victims. Who needs help first?

Victim 1 Infant unconscious on the floor. (There is a piggy bank near her and her face is lying on some coins that are scattered about.)

Victim 2 The 6-year old is lying on the floor screaming with a bookcase toppled over close to him. (He is holding his arm and has a cut on his head.)

Victim 3 The 4-year old is lying nearby with books, bookends, and some decorative glass figures tumbled around him. (He is bleeding from the head and crying.)

Emergency Situation—2

At a family party, two infants are put to sleep on a bed. When you go to check on them you find that both have either rolled or crept off onto the floor. You have two victims. Who needs help first?

Victim 1 The infant is crying and holding his arm at an unusual angle.

Victim 2 The infant appears unconscious but there is no blood or apparent deformity present.

Emergency Situation—3

On a busy street, a driver swerves to avoid a jaywalker and goes over the curb, coming to a stop on the sidewalk after hitting several people and knocking over 2 strollers, each with an infant strapped in.

Victim 1 A man was knocked down but is getting up again, appears dazed but not seriously injured.

Victim 2 The younger infant is slumped sideways in the stroller and appears unconscious.

Victim 3 The older infant is crying and bleeding from a cut on his arm.

Victim 4 A 3-year-old child is sitting on the pavement crying, but appears uninjured.

PRIORITIZING CARE—INFANT AND CHILD

Prioritizing Care Activity

In an emergency with more than one victim, you may need to prioritize care **(determine who needs help first)**.

Directions:

Read the following emergency situations. Circle the victim in each emergency situation who has a life-threatening condition and needs help first.

Emergency Situation—1

You are the first person to stop on a busy highway to assist at an accident scene. Who do you help first?

Victim 1 The driver who is calling for help but otherwise appears uninjured.

Victim 2 The infant in the back middle passenger seat of the car (in a car seat) who is not moving and appears to be unconscious.

Victim 3 The older child behind the mother who is crying and you see a small cut on his right lower leg.

Emergency Situation—2

Three children playing in a tree house in the backyard suddenly tumble to the ground when the tree house falls to one side. Who do you help first?

Victim 1 The child who has a gash on his forehead, which is bleeding.

Victim 2 The child who is crying and trying to remove her arm, which is trapped between boards, but does not appear to be bleeding.

Victim 3 The child who was hit by falling boards is lying quietly, appears unconscious, and is bleeding from a gash on his arm.

Emergency Situation—3

You go to a cafeteria for lunch. You see a young mother feeding her children when you hear a crash. Who needs help first?

Victim 1 The crying infant who fell from her high chair.

Victim 2 The infant looking panicked and clutching her throat.

Victim 3 The mother, who is bleeding from her hand.

AMERICAN RED CROSS INFANT AND CHILD CPR COURSE

Examination Answer Sheet

Name _____ Date _____

Course: ❑ Child CPR (Complete Sections 1 and 2)

❑ Infant CPR (Complete Sections 1 and 3)

❑ Infant and Child CPR (Complete Sections 1, 2, and 3)

Examination: Ⓐ

Section 1—Before Providing Care

1.	ⓐ	ⓑ	ⓒ	ⓓ
2.	ⓐ	ⓑ	ⓒ	ⓓ
3.	ⓐ	ⓑ	ⓒ	ⓓ
4.	ⓐ	ⓑ	ⓒ	ⓓ
5.	ⓐ	ⓑ	ⓒ	ⓓ
6.	ⓐ	ⓑ	ⓒ	ⓓ
7.	ⓐ	ⓑ	ⓒ	ⓓ
8.	ⓐ	ⓑ	ⓒ	ⓓ
9.	True/False			
10.	True/False			

Section 2—Child CPR

1.	ⓐ	ⓑ	ⓒ	ⓓ
2.	ⓐ	ⓑ	ⓒ	ⓓ
3.	ⓐ	ⓑ	ⓒ	ⓓ
4.	ⓐ	ⓑ	ⓒ	ⓓ
5.	ⓐ	ⓑ	ⓒ	ⓓ
6.	ⓐ	ⓑ	ⓒ	ⓓ
7.	ⓐ	ⓑ	ⓒ	ⓓ
8.	ⓐ	ⓑ	ⓒ	ⓓ
9.	ⓐ	ⓑ	ⓒ	ⓓ
10.	ⓐ	ⓑ	ⓒ	ⓓ

Section 3—Infant CPR

1.	ⓐ	ⓑ	ⓒ	ⓓ
2.	ⓐ	ⓑ	ⓒ	ⓓ
3.	ⓐ	ⓑ	ⓒ	ⓓ
4.	ⓐ	ⓑ	ⓒ	ⓓ
5.	ⓐ	ⓑ	ⓒ	ⓓ
6.	ⓐ	ⓑ	ⓒ	ⓓ
7.	ⓐ	ⓑ	ⓒ	ⓓ
8.	ⓐ	ⓑ	ⓒ	ⓓ
9.	ⓐ	ⓑ	ⓒ	ⓓ
10.	ⓐ	ⓑ	ⓒ	ⓓ

AMERICAN RED CROSS INFANT AND CHILD CPR COURSE

Examination Answer Sheet

Name _____ Date _____

Course:
- ❑ Child CPR (Complete Sections 1 and 2)
- ❑ Infant CPR (Complete Sections 1 and 3)
- ❑ Infant and Child CPR (Complete Sections 1, 2, and 3)

Examination: Ⓑ

Section 1—Before Providing Care

1.	ⓐ	ⓑ	ⓒ	ⓓ
2.	ⓐ	ⓑ	ⓒ	ⓓ
3.	ⓐ	ⓑ	ⓒ	ⓓ
4.	ⓐ	ⓑ	ⓒ	ⓓ
5.	ⓐ	ⓑ	ⓒ	ⓓ
6.	ⓐ	ⓑ	ⓒ	ⓓ
7.	ⓐ	ⓑ	ⓒ	ⓓ
8.	ⓐ	ⓑ	ⓒ	ⓓ
9.	True/False			
10.	True/False			

Section 2—Child CPR

1.	ⓐ	ⓑ	ⓒ	ⓓ
2.	ⓐ	ⓑ	ⓒ	ⓓ
3.	ⓐ	ⓑ	ⓒ	ⓓ
4.	ⓐ	ⓑ	ⓒ	ⓓ
5.	ⓐ	ⓑ	ⓒ	ⓓ
6.	ⓐ	ⓑ	ⓒ	ⓓ
7.	ⓐ	ⓑ	ⓒ	ⓓ
8.	ⓐ	ⓑ	ⓒ	ⓓ
9.	ⓐ	ⓑ	ⓒ	ⓓ
10.	ⓐ	ⓑ	ⓒ	ⓓ

Section 3—Infant CPR

1.	ⓐ	ⓑ	ⓒ	ⓓ
2.	ⓐ	ⓑ	ⓒ	ⓓ
3.	ⓐ	ⓑ	ⓒ	ⓓ
4.	ⓐ	ⓑ	ⓒ	ⓓ
5.	ⓐ	ⓑ	ⓒ	ⓓ
6.	ⓐ	ⓑ	ⓒ	ⓓ
7.	ⓐ	ⓑ	ⓒ	ⓓ
8.	ⓐ	ⓑ	ⓒ	ⓓ
9.	ⓐ	ⓑ	ⓒ	ⓓ
10.	ⓐ	ⓑ	ⓒ	ⓓ

AMERICAN RED CROSS INFANT AND CHILD CPR COURSE

Examination A

Instructions:

Read each question slowly and carefully. Then choose the best answer. Fill in that circle on the answer sheet on page 71. When you are done with the examination, hand in the completed answer sheet to your instructor.

Section 1—Before Providing Care

1. How can you protect yourself from disease transmission when giving care?
   a) Provide 2 rescue breaths with every 15 compressions.
   b) Wipe off the victim's hands and mouth.
   c) Use protective equipment, such as disposable gloves and breathing barriers, when giving care.
   d) Get annual physical exams after age 40.

2. The emergency action steps to follow are—
   a) Check-Call-Care.
   b) Check-Call-Secure.
   c) Check-Call-Defibrillate.
   d) Early access-Early CPR-Early recognition.

3. You are at the mall when you see what looks like a serious accident involving a bicycle and a vehicle. Why should you check the scene before giving care?
   a) To find out what happened and how many victims there are
   b) To ensure your own safety
   c) To see if there are any bystanders who can help
   d) All of the above

4. You respond to an emergency and find four victims. Which victim should you care for first?
   a) A victim who is bleeding slightly from his thigh
   b) A victim who is complaining of pain in his knee
   c) A victim who has a small burn on his fingertip
   d) A victim who is unconscious

5. You are on your lunch break when you notice a child who appears to be unconscious. After checking the scene, you check the child for consciousness by—
   a) Rolling him onto his side and sweeping his mouth.
   b) Checking his blood pressure.
   c) Gently tapping him and shouting, "Are you O.K.!"
   d) Checking for signs of circulation.

6. At a youth soccer game, you see a player collapse. You check the scene and then check the child for consciousness, but he does not respond. What should you do next?
   a) Have a bystander call 9-1-1 or the local emergency number.
   b) Give 5 rescue breaths.
   c) Give 2 back blows.
   d) Move the child.

7. What does the "C" in "A-B-C" stand for?
   a) Continue
   b) Circulation
   c) Compressions
   d) Choking

8. When checking for breathing in an unconscious child—
   a) Place the victim in the recovery position.
   b) Lift the head and tilt the chin.
   c) Pinch the victim's nose shut.
   d) Look, listen, and feel for breathing.

9. A child has a life-threatening condition. There is no parent or guardian present. Consent is implied, so you should provide care.

   True

   False

10. A child may have suffered a neck injury. There is no immediate danger to you or the child. You should move the victim to a comfortable position.

    True

    False

Not to be reproduced without permission.

Section 2—Child CPR

1. What is the purpose of CPR?
a) CPR restarts the heart.
b) With CPR, the child will not need advanced medical care.
c) CPR helps circulate blood containing oxygen to the vital organs until more advanced medical personnel arrive and take over.
d) CPR prevents a cardiac emergency.

2. You notice that a child looks panicked. (She cannot cough, speak, or breathe.) What life-threatening condition could the child be experiencing?
a) Indigestion
b) Cardiac arrest
c) Upset stomach
d) Choking

3. When giving rescue breaths to a child—
a) Give quick breaths at the rate of about 40 to 80 per minute.
b) Give about 5 compressions.
c) Give back blows and chest thrusts.
d) Take a breath and breathe slowly into the child, just enough to make the chest clearly rise.

4. When giving care to a child who is conscious and has an obstructed airway, where do you position your hand to give abdominal thrusts?
a) On the rib cage
b) Just above the belly button
c) In the center of the breastbone
d) Any of the above

5. When giving CPR—
a) Compress the chest straight down about $1 - 1^1/_2$ inches with one hand.
b) Give cycles of 5 chest compressions and 1 rescue breath.
c) Compress the chest at a 45-degree angle.
d) A and B.

6. Where do you place your hand to give chest compressions during child CPR?
a) One hand on the notch of the breastbone and the other on the nose to hold it open
b) One hand on the notch and one on the ribcage
c) One hand on the center of the breastbone, just above the notch where the ribs meet the breastbone
d) Over the stomach, just above the belly button and below the notch

7. Your child is choking on a french fry. When you reach the child, you ask if he is choking and he frantically nods his head yes. As you send someone to call 9-1-1, what should you do?
a) Try to give 2 rescue breaths.
b) Check his brachial pulse.
c) Give 15 chest compressions.
d) Stand behind the child and give abdominal thrusts.

8. When should you initially check a child for signs of circulation?
a) After giving 2 effective rescue breaths
b) After 15 chest compressions and 2 rescue breaths
c) About 4-5 minutes after you began CPR
d) After checking the scene for safety

9. When giving care to a child who is unconscious and has an obstructed airway, where do you position your hand to give compressions?
a) On the back sides of the rib cage
b) Below the belly button in the center of the abdomen
c) Above the belly button and below the notch where the ribs meet the breastbone
d) One hand on the center of the breastbone, just above the notch where the ribs meet the breastbone

10. To check if an unconscious child is breathing—
a) Check for the brachial pulse in the arm.
b) Look, listen, and feel for breathing.
c) Look in the victim's mouth for at least 10 seconds.
d) Place your hands on the rib cage to feel for chest expansion.

Section 3—Infant CPR

1. Some signs that an infant is choking are—
   a) Rapid breathing and crying.
   b) Looking panicked and not able to cough, cry, or breathe.
   c) Breathing noisily and deeply.
   d) Crying and spitting up food.

2. When giving rescue breaths to an infant—
   a) Give quick breaths at the rate of about 40 to 80 per minute.
   b) Give about 5 compressions.
   c) Give back blows and chest thrusts.
   d) Take a breath and breathe slowly into the infant, just enough to make the chest clearly rise.

3. When giving care to an infant who is unconscious and has an obstructed airway, where do you position your fingers to give chest compressions?
   a) On the rib cage
   b) On the breastbone near the neck
   c) In the center of the breastbone, one finger width below the nipple line
   d) Any of the above

4. When giving an infant CPR—
   a) Compress the chest straight down about $1/2$-1 inch with two fingers.
   b) Give cycles of 5 chest compressions and 1 rescue breath.
   c) Compress the chest at a 45-degree angle.
   d) A and B.

5. An infant in need of CPR will have—
   a) Rapid and shallow breathing.
   b) No breathing and no signs of circulation.
   c) Signs of circulation and will be conscious.
   d) Breathing and no signs of circulation.

6. Where do you place your fingers to give chest compressions during infant CPR?
   a) Two fingers on the notch of the breastbone and on the nose to hold it open
   b) Two fingers on the notch and one on the ribcage
   c) The heel of one hand on the center of the breastbone, just below the nipple line
   d) Two fingers on the center of the breastbone, one finger width below the nipple line

7. You are in a fast food restaurant when your conscious 11-month-old infant chokes on a french fry and is unable to breathe. As you send someone to call 9-1-1, what should you do?
   a) Try to give 2 rescue breaths.
   b) Check for signs of circulation.
   c) Give back blows and chest thrusts.
   d) Stand behind the infant and give abdominal thrusts.

8. When should you initially check an infant for signs of circulation?
   a) After giving 2 effective rescue breaths
   b) After 15 chest compressions and 2 rescue breaths
   c) About 4-5 minutes after you began CPR
   d) After checking the scene for safety

9. When giving care to an infant who is conscious and choking, where do you position your hand for back blows?
   a) On the back sides of the rib cage
   b) Below the belly button
   c) In the middle of the back, between the shoulder blades
   d) Any of the above

10. To check if an unconscious infant is breathing—
    a) Check for the carotid pulse in the neck.
    b) Look, listen, and feel for breathing.
    c) Look in the infant's mouth for at least 10 seconds.
    d) Hold your hands over the rib cage to feel for chest expansion.

AMERICAN RED CROSS INFANT AND CHILD CPR COURSE

Examination B

Instructions:

Read each question slowly and carefully. Then choose the best answer.
Fill in that circle on the answer sheet on page 73. When you are done
with the examination, hand in the completed answer sheet to your instructor.

Section 1—Before Providing Care

1. When checking for breathing in an unconscious child—
a) Place the victim in the recovery position.
b) Lift the head and tilt the chin.
c) Pinch the victim's nose shut.
d) Look, listen, and feel for breathing.

2. You are at the mall when you see what looks like a serious accident involving a bicycle and a vehicle. Why should you check the scene before giving care?
a) To find out what happened and how many victims there are
b) To ensure your own safety
c) To see if there are any bystanders who can help
d) All of the above

3. You respond to an emergency and find four victims. Which victim should you care for first?
a) A victim who is bleeding slightly from his thigh
b) A victim who is complaining of pain in his knee
c) A victim who has a small burn on his fingertip
d) A victim who is unconscious

4. The emergency action steps to follow are—
a) Check-Call-Care.
b) Check-Call-Secure.
c) Check-Call-Defibrillate.
d) Early access-Early CPR-Early recognition.

5. How can you protect yourself from disease transmission when giving care?
a) Provide 2 rescue breaths with every 15 compressions.
b) Wipe off the victim's mouth and hands.
c) Use protective equipment, such as disposable gloves and breathing barriers, when giving care.
d) Get annual physical exams after age 40.

6. What does the "C" in "A-B-C" stand for?
a) Continue
b) Circulation
c) Compressions
d) Choking

7. At a youth soccer game, you see a player collapse. You check the scene and then check the child for consciousness, but he does not respond. What should you do next?
a) Have a bystander call 9-1-1 or the local emergency number.
b) Give abdominal thrusts.
c) Check for signs of circulation.
d) Move the child.

8. You are on your lunch break when you notice a child who appears to be unconscious. After checking the scene, you check the child for consciousness by—
a) Rolling him onto his side and sweeping his mouth.
b) Checking his blood pressure.
c) Gently tapping him and shouting, "Are you O.K.!"
d) Checking for signs of circulation.

9. A child may have suffered a neck injury. There is no immediate danger to you or the child. You should move the victim to a comfortable position.

True

False

10. A child has a life-threatening condition. There is no parent or guardian present. Consent is implied, so you should provide care.

True

False

Section 2—Child CPR

1. You are in a fast food restaurant when you see a child, who was playing with french fries in his mouth and running, suddenly clutch his throat with both hands. When you reach the child, you ask if he is choking and he frantically nods his head yes. You inform the parents that you are trained in first aid and can help; they give you permission. As you send someone to call 9-1-1, what should you do?

a) Try to give 2 rescue breaths.

b) Check his brachial pulse.

c) Give 15 chest compressions.

d) Stand behind the child and give abdominal thrusts.

2. When giving care to a child who is unconscious and has an obstructed airway, where do you position your hand to give chest compressions?

a) On the rib cage

b) On the belly button

c) In the center of the breastbone

d) Any of the above

3. When giving care to a child who is conscious and has an obstructed airway, where do you position your hands to give abdominal thrusts?

a) On the backsides of the rib cage

b) Below the belly button in the center of the abdomen

c) One hand on the center of the breastbone, just above the notch where the ribs meet the breastbone, and the other on the forehead

d) Above the belly button and below the notch where the ribs meet the breastbone

4. What is the purpose of CPR?

a) CPR restarts the heart.

b) With CPR, the child will not need advanced medical care.

c) CPR helps circulate blood containing oxygen to the vital organs until more advanced medical personnel arrive and take over.

d) CPR prevents a cardiac emergency.

5. Where do you place your hands to give chest compressions during child CPR?

a) One hand on the notch of the breastbone and the other on the nose to hold it open

b) One hand on the notch and one on the ribcage

c) One hand on the center of the breastbone, just above the notch where the ribs meet the breastbone, and the other on the forehead

d) Over the stomach, just above the belly button and below the notch

6. To check if an unconscious child is breathing—

a) Check for the brachial pulse in the arm.

b) Look, listen, and feel for breathing.

c) Look in the victim's mouth for at least 10 seconds.

d) Place your hands on the rib cage to feel for chest expansion.

7. When giving rescue breaths to a child—

a) Give quick breaths at the rate of about 40 to 80 per minute.

b) Give about 5 compressions.

c) Give back blows and chest thrusts.

d) Take a breath and breathe slowly into the child, just enough to make the chest clearly rise.

8. When giving a child CPR—

a) Compress the chest straight down about 1 to $1^1/_2$ inches with one hand.

b) Give cycles of 5 chest compressions and 1 rescue breath.

c) Compress the chest at a 45-degree angle.

d) A and B.

9. When should you initially check a child for signs of circulation?

a) After giving 2 effective rescue breaths

b) After 15 chest compressions and 2 rescue breaths

c) About 4-5 minutes after you began CPR

d) After checking the scene for safety

10. You notice that a child looks panicked. (She cannot cough, speak, or breathe.) What life-threatening condition could the child be experiencing?

a) Indigestion

b) Cardiac arrest

c) Upset stomach

d) Choking

Section 3—Infant CPR

1. An infant in need of CPR will have—
a) Rapid and shallow breathing.
b) No breathing and no signs of circulation.
c) Signs of circulation and will be conscious.
d) Breathing and no signs of circulation.

2. Some signs that an infant is choking are—
a) Looking panicked and not able to not cough, cry, or breathe.
b) Rapid, shallow breathing and crying.
c) Breathing noisily and deeply.
d) Crying and spitting up food.

3. Where do you place your fingers to give chest compressions during infant CPR?
a) Two fingers on the notch of the breastbone and on the nose to hold it open
b) Two fingers on the notch and one on the ribcage
c) The heel of one hand on the center of the breastbone, just below the nipple line
d) Two fingers on the center of the breastbone one-finger width below the nipple line

4. When giving care to an infant who is unconscious and has an obstructed airway, where do you position your fingers to give chest compressions?
a) On the belly button
b) At the top of the breastbone near the neck
c) In the center of the breastbone, one finger width below the nipple line
d) Any of the above

5. Your conscious 11-month-old infant chokes on a french fry. As you send someone to call 9-1-1, what should you do?
a) Try to give 2 rescue breaths
b) Check for signs of circulation
c) Give 5 back blows and 5 chest thrusts
d) Stand behind the infant and give abdominal thrusts

6. When should you initially check an infant for signs of circulation?
a) After giving 2 effective rescue breaths
b) After 15 chest compressions and 2 rescue breaths
c) About 4-5 minutes after you began CPR
d) After checking the scene for safety

7. When giving care to an infant who is conscious and has an obstructed airway, where do you position your hand for back blows?
a) On the backsides of the rib cage
b) Below the belly button
c) In the middle of the back, between the shoulder blades
d) Any of the above

8. To check if an unconscious infant is breathing—
a) Check for the carotid pulse in the neck.
b) Look, listen, and feel for breathing.
c) Look in the infant's mouth for at least 10 seconds.
d) Hold your hands over the rib cage to feel for chest expansion.

9. When giving rescue breaths to an infant—
a) Give quick breaths at the rate of about 40 to 80 per minute.
b) Give about 5 compressions.
c) Give back blows and chest thrusts.
d) Take a breath and breathe slowly into the infant; just enough to make the chest clearly rise.

10. When giving an infant CPR—
a) Compress the chest straight down about $1/2$ to 1 inch with two fingers.
b) Give cycles of 5 chest compressions and 1 rescue breath.
c) Compress the chest at a 45-degree angle.
d) A and B.